Hope for A New Era

*Turning the Tide: Love & Leadership
Through Turbulent Times*

Cynthia Rivard

ISBN 978-1-967953-00-4

Published by Global Rising Tide Foundation

www.globalrisingtide.org
www.cynthiarivard.com

Dedication

With love and gratitude for my family.
Jim, Michaela, Jared, Daniel and Jamie -
You help me stay grounded and remember
why this work is so important.

You inspire me every day to be better and
do more… to never give up or waiver from
this cause of helping to create a better future,
so that you have one.

All proceeds benefit the
Global Rising Tide Foundation

Content

Prologue

I have a confession to make. I am very aware and focused on making my teachings relevant to the student, and so I tend to share very little of my personal details. It is not about me.

Because of the number of questions I receive about my origin story, however, I would like to provide a bit more context for those who are curious. Not only is it helpful to know more about the person you are learning from, but I hope it will also inspire some of you to understand that a more fulfilling path is available to you as well. You will recognize how it is never too late in your life's journey to make a life changing pivot, or expand your life's work in a significant way.

Each and every one of you who has been compelled to pick-up this book was guided to it for a reason. Your awareness is meant to continue to grow and with it your impact, as you learn to recognize and follow your guidance. Trust me when I say that I was the least likely of candidates for this journey that I am now on...

I had an unremarkable upbringing in a middle class family, growing up in the United States, in the suburbs of Washington, D.C. Similar to many of my generation (born in the 60's), I was the victim of significant emotional abuse and trauma. It was no one's fault, because it was the endorsed, prevalent parenting style of that time. My mother had also been emotionally abused, so it was all she knew about how to parent. She had a big heart and I suppressed most of those unhappy memories, feeling guilty for holding any less than loyal and loving emotions for her.

But the lessons and subconscious beliefs that formed in my childhood influenced my behavior for decades. I had developed an extreme lack of self-love, esteem and confidence, although I learned to mask my insecurities and came across as a secure leader. I was compelled to overachieve, due to desperately wanting approval from others and to prove my worth to myself. We will talk about this concept in the coming chapters because a lack of self-love is pervasive in our societies. It is not obvious to most who suffer from it, but it holds them back from living their most abundantly happy and fulfilled lives.

I went on from being an overachiever in school, to losing myself in work that I enjoyed but never found real fulfillment in. I learned and grew in leadership roles and seemed to have an innate ability in this area which served me well. It was in fact extremely helpful, since my ego was too fragile to consciously look for weaknesses and intentionally strive to improve them. If you have ever struggled with self-worth, this should resonate with you. It is a significant issue holding most people back. We have to be able to view our weak areas objectively, in order to grow and improve them; and we are meant to learn, grow and evolve as "better humans" throughout our lives. Lack of self-love is a pandemic of massive proportions that few currently recognize or seek to cure; and it is a major contributor to the current mess in our world, but I digress.

I moved on from college and my early career years to Boston, and then to the island of Martha's Vineyard following career opportunities. As it turned out, the island was my last move for work. I did not recognize it at the time, but my guidance had intentionally led me there. I was destined to meet my soulmate on Martha's Vineyard, as well as raise our four children in an environment conducive to learning, community connection and environmental awareness.

Martha's Vineyard has an unwarranted, bad reputation. It has been spun as the playground for presidents and the elite, when in fact it hosts a vibrant and heart centered year round population. Most members of that community are not wealthy in the financial sense; but I believe many are wealthy in their connection to nature and community. A large part of the first world population has lost its connection to the earth, and I did not fully appreciate how unique the holistic environment there was. There are other communities like this, of course, but it is sadly not yet the norm.

The affluent residents of that island have been villainized, and I feel compelled to call attention to the fact that money does not make someone bad. Greed does. What I saw in that community was an abundance of philanthropy that kept it alive and thriving, along with the love and compassion for neighbors that proliferated. It is not a coincidence that the island has a higher vibration than most places on the planet.

"So how did you become a channel," you may be wondering?

This is the part where I am obliged to point out that there is no "right" time to spiritually awaken and there is no phase in life that should be considered too late. I had a busy life and was very much asleep for the better part of six decades.

As a mom of four and executive working more than full time, there was no wiggle room in my schedule to think about anything I deemed to be nonessential. Under a blanket of chronic stress from juggling it all, I did not prioritize my spirituality. I took my children to church for a while because it had been part of my upbringing, but I felt disconnected from a Higher Power and knew church was not the answer for me. I did not know where else to look, however; and I definitely did not believe I had the bandwidth at that time in my life to figure it out.

I am now aware that all of that busyness was part of the divine plan to keep me asleep for that chapter of my life. Honing my leadership skills and raising my children were my purpose during that period. It was not yet time to become aware or take action on my main life's purpose.

Many of you may find yourself in a similar place, regardless of your age. You were guided to this book and the opening or expanding of your awareness because this is your time. Stay curious and keep following those nudges. We are in tremendously turbulent times and there is much changing, and needing to transition in the world. And you will be called to help in new or expanded ways. I will focus more on this in the coming chapters.

Spiritual awakening is not nearly as mysterious or unavailable as I was led to believe. It is merely learning how to receive communication from the Divine, and then honing that skill. And this is easy to do once you become intentional about it.

I was unaware of my spiritual awakening, that is how easy it was. There was so much I did not know and my lack of spiritual awareness was also part of the divine plan for my life. There are many distortions and an abundance of misinformation in religious and new age teachings, proliferated by those who unknowingly pass on what they were wrongly taught, which compounds the misunderstandings. My guidance ensured that I did not fall victim to misinformation by becoming curious too early. I was meant to learn the simple truth from my own inner wisdom.

If you are wanting more details on the "how," I will say that I followed a series of bread crumbs, led by what many would describe as intuition and synchronicities. I became curious and turned over a few rocks that I came upon, which led me in new directions. If you are new to this topic, I share some easy ways to get started on this book's resources web page.[1]

Our inner wisdom is how we are all meant to glean the truth. I intend that this book will open your awareness to all of the possibilities, and then you look within to ensure that it resonates; because the truth lies within you, too.

I did not realize until very recently that I was now awake or that I was "channeling". Those were scary concepts for me, that would have had me running for cover a few years ago; but as it turns out, channeling is simply receiving communication from Divinity or your inner wisdom. Most already receive this type of communication occasionally and call it intuition, but in the majority of those cases it is actually claircognizance.

Clair senses, also known as the sixth sense, are the ways we are able to receive communication from Divinity. As my clairs became stronger, my faith in the very clear guidance that I was receiving flourished. I have recently been led down many new paths that were nowhere on my radar a couple of years ago. Being an author is one of them, as well as being an energy master and nonprofit founder.

By the way, that self-love and esteem deficit that I mentioned from my earlier years did not completely resolve itself until I spiritually awakened. It is one thing to understand conceptually that God or Spirit is in each of us and that we are worthy, and it is quite another to KNOW it in your heart. Arriving at that place of knowing is profound, and allowed me to move past all of my self-sabotaging, "I'm not good enough" behaviors. In essence, my guidance would no longer allow me to continue playing small.

This is another powerful lesson that I hope you are open to receiving. You have more greatness in you than you can possibly know, until you develop that clear communication channel. Your inner guidance may challenge you to think and act differently and get up to things you never thought were possible, but you would not be given the idea if it was not your path to explore it.

And when you know and trust that you are divinely guided, the typical fear of doing something new or different dissipates. You will know that no matter how different the ideas or actions seem or how many times you hit an obstacle, you are doing what is needed to traverse your soul's path and co-create your most fulfilled life.

Introduction

The earth is a very special place. Its beauty is breathtaking and God's glory can be seen daily in the sun rising and setting. We see it in the magnificence of a wild animal spotted on the horizon, and can hear it in the music of birds that most tune out as background noise. Or that we allow to be drowned out by a cacophony of traffic noise and too loud music.

We are surrounded by the magic of creation but the majority of inhabitants in our first world nations do not slow down long enough to appreciate it. In fact, most not only take it for granted, but unknowingly contribute to its destruction through their daily partnerships with toxic companies.

As a species, we have a responsibility to care for and steward the earth and all of its creatures; but very few people in our modern world are fully aware of their role and responsibility in ensuring the continuation of life on our planet. Many do not yet comprehend how they are meant to uphold this critical obligation.

In reality, the majority of populations around the globe have done the opposite. It has become an accepted practice to abuse the planet's natural resources and the precious lives of its creatures.

Deforestation is rampant.[2] The use of wood is a norm with little thought given to replenishing it; subsequently the critical oxygen supply that the trees give us and that sustains human life continues to decline.

The widespread use of fossil fuels continues to increase rather than decline, even after decades of warnings about the Greenhouse Effect.[3]

The toxins in our air, water and the majority of our food and products are at an all time high, contributing to an escalating health crisis and mortality rates.

The masses can no longer stay silent while assuming the politicians of the world are going to agree and implement a strategy to save us.

Like many of you, I used to hold the opinion that my one voice or actions could not make much difference. Who was I to be able to contribute to the complex solutions that are needed? Surely the brightest and best minds on the planet have this covered…

Except they do not.

The voices of informed scientists, well meaning politicians and environmental advocates are not enough. They are being drowned out by the deafening denials of the greedy and selfish who do not want anything to disrupt their profits or current conveniences.

When my claircognizance became clear, I was given reassurance and clarity on the truth my heart already knew... that my voice (and yours) really can, and is meant to make a difference.

Leadership is an ability to influence others, which we all wield in our own unique ways. You may influence your children or other family members or friends on a daily basis.

You may influence your co-workers through your energy or the information that you share. You may participate in community based projects, school, sports or religious groups where you meet and communicate with others.

You may share thoughts on social media.

Anywhere you communicate, you have an ability to influence others which cannot be taken lightly. Each of us has a responsibility to influence those we can, in meaningful and supportive ways.

As the world's government officials continue to argue over whether global warming really exists, the planet is being destroyed along with our future and the potential of a future for our children.

The message in this book came from my inner wisdom. The urgency that I speak about cannot be found in current scientific statistical projections because our trajectory is accelerating too fast for scientists' predictions to keep up to it. And so I have been guided *to sound the alarm,* along with sharing this message of hope.

Our current reality calls for us to take immediate and massive action.

Divinity has also shared the promise of a beautiful future for humanity. A new golden era is waiting for us.

It will not magically materialize, however. We have to work to create it.

And we must start by taking responsibility for our past actions and the devastation we have wreaked on the planet as a global collective.

And that will necessitate substantive change.

Life is defined by our perspectives and beliefs.

They create who we become. They create our thoughts and how we interact with others.

And none of it is real. It is all an illusion based on our childhood programming.

When we discover the beauty of new perspectives, our world opens up. We develop more compassion and experience more love and peace.

This treatise will explain the power of the shift.

It explains what will happen when we open to new ways of being, thinking and relating.

We each have just a short time on this planet to evolve ourselves and to love and help others.

This is the only reason we are here.

We are meant to love unconditionally and to steward our planet and all of her animals and resources. Regardless of our backgrounds and the perspectives we were burdened with growing up, we can each still make this way of being *our way now*.

Programming can be changed or overwritten.It is all a choice that can be made consciously.

Our planet needs each one of us to become aware of our plight, shift our perspectives and prioritize peace and our environment in big, trajectory shifting ways.

I intend for this book to be a call to action, along with seeding hope and the start of a peaceful revolution.

As they might have said in "Star Wars"... *We are our planet's only hope.*

Standing with you in action for our future,

Cynthia

Improvement is possible when we take responsibility for our choices that helped to create the undesired circumstance.

The Three R's - Reality, Responsibility & Revolution

The world is a troubled, turbulent place. It has been for the majority of mankind's existence, but our current reality is the most globally violent and destructive time in human history.

Yes, there is the bombardment of global media coverage that makes us more aware of tragedies of war or horrific weather events that may be happening on the other side of the planet.

But there is also a world wide uptick in conflict and chaos.

As a global community we are witness to more dissension than at any other time in our history; and climate change has produced a cascade of disastrous weather, the likes of which the planet has never seen.

It is a harsh and disheartening reality. Some are prophesying the end of the world; and if we choose to ignore all of the warnings of catastrophe, we will be electing to allow it.

Discerning Your Truth

Along with a lot of actionable information and strategies to implement, I am going to share some potentially new ideas with you that you may find hard to believe. I don't expect or want anyone to believe anything they read here.

My intention is to open your awareness to new possibilities and paradigms. Do not reject new-to-you information immediately. Just allow it to be in your awareness.

We will talk repeatedly about being open to new concepts and/or adopting new behaviors, and the importance of gleaning your own soul's path and truth.

Do not accept anything you hear at face value, whether it comes from the media, government authorities, other authority figures or friends. It is important to the future of humanity that everyone learns how to discern their own truth.

And that truth lies within you.

Inherent in understanding your inner truth, is fostering a communication channel with Divinity. When I talk about this topic, it is not from a "new age" perspective but from timeless principles that form a golden thread throughout all of the world's religions. No matter what you believe and the words you use in your practice, you can mentally substitute your words and apply these principles to your existing belief systems. This epitaph is not attempting to rip away the structure of your belief systems, but to wrap you in a warm blanket of assurance that it all can work together when you stay open to new ideas.

The Nature of Spirituality

Before my own spiritual awakening, I misunderstood this term and would like to clarify a definition for our use moving forward.

Spirituality is your personal relationship with Spirit (or God/Allah).

That's it.

It does not matter what religion you believe in or what practices you have adopted. It does not matter how you pray or if you pray.

A relationship implies a back and forth, meaning that there are two parties or components involved. Most people practice spirituality through prayer, which is just a one way communication.

In order to be in a relationship with our Great Creator, **you must listen** and allow God to communicate with you.

This is all that spirituality is; but it is foundational to who we are as humans.

God wants a two-way relationship with us, and for us to know their love.

And the only way to truly know their love is by developing your inner wisdom. Your inner truth or knowing is referred to by many different words. Some call it intuition, inner wisdom or guidance from God. It is actually your communication channel, or claircognizance, for receiving God's guidance.[4]

It is paramount to our collective success in creating a better world that each of us is able to receive and act on our guidance, which is unique to us. So I encourage you to explore honing your skill of claircognizance further. It is not a special gift as many assume. It is something everyone is able and meant to develop.

There are many instances when having strong communication or guidance from Divinity can be in your highest good. In fact, I would contend that it can help in every choice or decision you make, throughout your life.

Your guidance is meant to be your compass and steer you away from the distractions and misdirections that life can present. It will be your north star, keeping you on your soul's path and supporting you in living your purpose and most fulfilled life. It will guide you through taking the most aligned actions, in order to have the most positive impact in both your life and those you are meant to support.

When I was guided to write this book, it was clear that it was time to pivot and align with my soul's ultimate purpose. My life up until this point has been my path, and a secondary purpose. It was a long path with many things I was meant to learn and people I was meant to meet and interact with along my journey. But it was not my primary purpose. That had to wait because the world was not yet ready for what I was here to share.

Part of my purpose is to spread a life affirming message of love and consciousness expansion. I was not guided to do this sooner because the world was not ready to receive it. Of course being ready is a subjective concept; and although many still are not ready to hear this message, we are out of time to wait.

Now is our time to expand and herald in a new and golden era of raised consciousness and unconditional love.

We are on the cusp of a beautiful next chapter in humanity's evolution, and we each have the opportunity to help bring it into fruition.

A Harbinger of Spring

Before a new beginning, however, there needs to be an end. The turbulence that we are currently experiencing can be seen as a harbinger of the spring and "rebirth" of humanity.

We are in the midst of a tumultuous ending of the most toxic and irresponsible chapter of mankind; and in the wake of the desolation will be a beautiful new era… If we choose to create it.

We each have free choice, and with choice comes responsibility.

Many of the world's most devoutly religious are expecting God to save us, but everything in the cosmos is ruled by Divine Law.

Of course God wants the best for us and this beautiful planet they created, but we have to take some responsibility for our actions and help co-create our vision of a better world.

The Law of Creation is a universal law which means that it governs the creation of everything in the cosmos, including the creation of our beautiful future. Two of the important precepts of the Law of Creation that must be in place in order to create anything is an aligned identity and aligned action taking.

This means we have to actively participate in the process of creating our next chapter.

It is God's plan for us to move into a next chapter for humanity that nurtures mankind and the planet; but this vision is not going to be handed to us like a magic bunny out of a hat trick. Working with Divine Law, including the universal Law of Creation, *we have to take responsibility for manifesting a golden new era, in order to create it.*

The changes that are necessary are calling forward a new breed of conscious leaders from around the globe. We will not improve our circumstances by sitting on our hands or dreaming and visioning from our couches. These turbulent times are serving to activate newly aware, visionary leaders. It is calling forward those with open hearts and minds who are willing to orchestrate outcomes that are for the good of all, rather than the wealth or convenience of a select few.

It will require a growing number of concerned citizens, as they become aware of problems needing solutions, to step forward and do something different.

This means embracing our identities as leaders for the new era and this next chapter of humanity.

It means putting aside family or cultural expectations and becoming vocal spokespersons for saving our planet and stewarding all of God's creations.

It is time for us to unite as global citizens and conscious leaders, to incite the peaceful revolution we must create to survive.

This is our time.

If you were compelled to pick-up this book, you are meant to help. Our future needs each of us to help in new or expanded ways.

Know you are never alone. God is always
with you, guiding you when you listen.

God's Promise

It has been promised throughout time, that humanity will eventually be led into a golden age. This spiritual concept is referred to in new age nomenclature as the New Earth. Christians and Jews look forward to it as a paradise or heaven on earth, Muslims seek to reach Jannah and Buddhists seek Nirvana.

If you research these concepts they are fairly similar, although some refer to experiencing this great joy in our current 3D existence and some believe we have to wait for the afterlife.

All of the major religions accurately portray Divinity's promise of a better future, except for one critical component. No matter how devout or good each of us has been, this better existence will not be delivered to us without additional work as a collective global community. The idea that it will be miraculously handed to us is a misinterpretation of how the Law of Creation works.

Divinity is always with us and is supplying us with the guidance necessary for us to navigate out of our misery and suffering. Their intention is to help us evolve out of this prison of dense, negative human emotions; and help us begin to reverse the more recent devastation we have created through carbon emissions.

The guidance is already available to us. It requires us to take responsibility for our current circumstances and to take action to create our dream of a better world. We must awaken to the reality of the mess we have created and work diligently to turn our current destructive trajectory around.

The best place for you to start is by developing your personal connection and relationship with God or Spirit. This will enable you to receive the clear guidance needed for you to know how to contribute to this necessary transition of our world. Each of us will need to do our part, to ensure that collectively we are able to create the promised golden era.

As a conscious global community, we must also own the responsibility that comes with advancing technology. The more science advances, the more potential pitfalls will present. Modernization and technology are good things for a variety of reasons; but they can also lead to destruction and the extinction of our species.

Humans can be selfish or shortsighted. As we develop advancing technologies, we must learn to honor the great responsibility we have to the rest of humanity.

There are so many benefits that have come from the innovations of our modern times, but we also invented the atom bomb which could have led to the end of humanity. Everything on the planet is interconnected through energy and delicate ecosystems. The reverberations from the devastation created by an atom bomb are enough to decimate the entire planet.

Human ingenuity and compassion will eventually end hunger and illness on the planet; but it is also human ingenuity that created the COVID-19 virus.. The deadly virus could have annihilated the planet due to the speed with which it mutated and rendered vaccines ineffective. It was the mutations becoming less viral and less fatal over time that saved us from being destroyed.

We can and must limit the scope of the pain and suffering of humanity's current conditions by **taking responsibility for it** and **guided action to reverse our course.**

A New Era

As mentioned, there is a golden thread of truth shared throughout all of the beliefs and world's religions, around the concept of a new era or desired state of being.

But because God's promise has been repeated and shared in various formats across millennia, it is natural that the message became distorted in a few ways.

This new era is not waiting for us on a different planet or plain of existence. It is not in a different dimension, and it is not something that we have to die to experience.

It also is not a special place that is available to only those holding specific beliefs or who have behaved in particular ways.

There is no need to earn a reward in God's eyes, limiting paradise to a select few. We are all God's creations, made in their image but imperfect by the nature of our humanity.

There is no one unworthy of God's love and enjoying the transcendent joy of what will be a new and golden era for humanity.

No one will be left behind.

I do not know about you, but I was relieved to hear this. My understanding of our loving God did not allow for filtering out those who have yet to come around on their journey to knowing Divinity. After all, there is always hope for new possibilities and an ability to make new choices tomorrow.

I will refer to the new era and beautiful possibilities for our future as humanity's next stage of evolution because that is exactly what it is. And there are **two distinct elements** to this next phase - this promised golden era - that are important to understand.

- The first is the individual experience. It requires the intentional action by each person to raise their consciousness and experience transcendent joy.

- The second will be our evolving systems and structures that impact the entire planet and will support humanity into the future.

A new era is possible and these two aspects of our next chapter of evolution are interconnected.

As we each work to raise our frequency and consciousness, we will become more aware of the divine guidance and inspiration that is always there for us. And as we recognize this inner wisdom, it will become easier to discern the actions necessary to create the new systems and structures our world needs.

Each of us as individuals will not understand all that will be necessary, of course; but as you connect with your own guidance and lean into your evolving path and purpose, *you will manifest your part of the bigger picture.*

Divinity has already assisted us with the path for our individual evolution. The vibration of the earth has already begun to increase, which allows for the most heavy, dense human emotions (i.e. - the unpleasant ones like anger, fear and hate) to be diffused more easily.[5]

The individual frequencies that are available to humans also expanded exponentially in 2023. For those availing themselves of these higher frequencies, it will become easier for them to develop a raised consciousness, which is the ultimate goal in order to experience transcendent joy, Nirvana or paradise on earth.[6]

Raising Consciousness

To be clear for our purposes, the definition of a raised consciousness is an awareness and frequency in the area of the higher vibrational emotions such as happiness, love and joy. Inner peace is also a higher frequency which you may have heard Buddhists refer to as the goal they aspire to achieve.

First you must raise your frequency, and as you do, it becomes easier to raise your consciousness. Achieving a raised consciousness will not mean that you no longer experience a range of emotions, however. Humans are emotional creatures and it is a part of being human to experience a range of emotions.

But as your consciousness rises, the swing of emotions on the lower extreme will lessen in depth and frequency. You will become skilled at experiencing the higher frequency, more pleasant emotions with more regularity and for longer periods.

Because of the expanded frequencies now available, this experience of a raised consciousness is available to each of us now. So in some respects, you may view our current reality as already having arrived at the next stage of our evolution.

This is only one aspect of the Golden Era, however. There is currently significant conflict and suffering in the world, due to the majority of the population still living in resonance with the lower frequency emotions.

Beyond helping more people raise their frequency, there is much for us to do in rebuilding systems and structures that will nurture and support humanity. It is this work and the necessary restructuring to create our golden era on a global scale that we will focus on in the subsequent chapters.

The personal joy and love that we are meant to experience as part of our promised next chapter is already available to you, however.

This is our time.

But each individual must choose to actively participate by aligning to the highest frequency available to them, in order to enjoy it.

The highest frequency that is available to you is referred to as your highest ascension point. This is the highest vibration that you are meant to reach in your lifetime. For everyone reading this, your goal should be to reach a frequency of 500 million bio-energy units which is the frequency of joy.[7]

Many have misunderstood the benefit of having a "high vibe" and how to have one.

The Law and Nature of Vibration

Because there are a lot of assumptions made with these terms, I am going to cover some foundational information to ensure there are no misunderstandings when we refer to them.

Everything is energy. Whether you can physically see it or not, energy is everywhere and everything is energy. The air we breathe, our thoughts and emotions, sound waves and other forms of electromagnetic transmissions are all energy. And energy vibrates. This is the Law of Vibration.

The speed or pattern that something vibrates at is known as its frequency and is the measurement used when we quantify the speed of vibration. Something with a slower vibration is denser and the absolute lowest frequencies can be seen as matter. Higher frequencies can not be seen and the highest of frequencies is known as the Akashic Field, which is the frequency of divine consciousness.

The frequency of human emotions and consciousness can be measured in bio-energy units. As explained earlier, the lower emotional frequencies are the dense, heaviest and most unpleasant of human emotions such as anger and greed; and at the other end of the emotional frequency scale are the higher frequencies of love, joy and inner peace.

Beyond the frequency that each of our cells vibrate at, each human body holds a prevalent emotional frequency because humans are emotional creatures. We can not be conscious without feeling an emotion, because our thoughts continuously create our emotional state.

Your thoughts create your emotions but your transitory

emotions do not create your personal vibration. *They will be influenced by it, however.* A higher vibration will help you experience the higher frequency emotions more often and hold them for longer periods. Because your thoughts create your emotions, managing your thoughts is a part of the process of raising your consciousness, and becomes easier as you come into resonance with those higher vibrational emotions.

A higher vibration has to come first and the 2023 expansion of the emotional frequency field makes it easier for us to raise our vibration and subsequently raise our consciousness.

A raised consciousness, for those who choose to develop it, will allow them to experience more joy and love along with benevolence toward the rest of humanity.

It will open the door to global cooperation and peace, and the ending of world poverty.

There have been individuals such as Jesus and Buddha who have achieved a raised consciousness in the past, but it was not possible for most of mankind.

The differentiator now is that the raised frequencies of the planet and human emotional frequency field are allowing for a raised consciousness to be attainable for everyone who chooses to develop it.

And as your frequency rises, you will have the additional benefit of more clear inner wisdom or guidance. This is a skill to develop; but it is much easier to hone at the higher frequencies, as you move closer to the frequency of Divinity.

When a pivotal percentage of the global collective's vibration becomes raised, there will be an abundance of people who are divinely guided in creating the systems and structures necessary to support humanity.

This will be the tide's turning point, when people around the globe will see the outward reflection of a new golden era. There is much work that will need to take place before this happens, however. How long it takes is up to us.

More of the world's population will embrace working toward this vision as they come into resonance with the frequency and consciousness of unconditional love.*

The new era will be a time and place where everyone will feel safe and no one will go hungry or cold.

Everyone will be able to experience the higher frequency emotions of unconditional love and joy.

There will be no violence or war.

There will be no greed or hoarding of the earth's abundant resources.

The new era will be a world full of peace and unconditional love.

THAT is Nirvana.

That IS heaven on earth.

* This does not imply that the earth's entire populace will need to raise their frequency and consciousness. That will not happen for several generations, as babies are born into the new raised frequencies. There will be many in the existing population who refuse to participate and will never experience this beautiful way of being.

A pivotal number to turn the tide will be approximately ten percent of the globe's population. This is a lot of people, but not an unachievable goal.

Love is a privilege and a responsibility
of being human.

A Call for Unconditional Love

Our souls are made to love.

Because God is love and light and in all things, love is the very fabric of the universe.

It is the lack of love we hold for our fellow humans and God's green earth that has led to our current predicament and the dangerous precipice we are teetering on.

We are out of equilibrium. When there is love, conflict, greed and selfishness disappear and everything moves into harmony and balance.

But that is not the path we are on at the moment. As a species, humans have lost sight of what is important.

Yes, there are some people in the world who embrace

love as their way, but the subsequent impact of these beautiful souls is minimal.

The World is Hurting

We are hovering on the edge of destruction. We are embroiled in an avoidable crisis caused by a lack of compassion in leadership and the unwillingness of earth's citizens to listen and allow other people's perspectives.

They do not view themselves as closed minded of course. Everyone believes that it is everyone else that is to blame.

But if more people were willing to really listen to each other, it would quiet the deafening roar of controversy and conflict.

It would allow for consensus building and the creation of plans that will be for the good of humanity. It would end the proliferation of behaviors and industries that benefit a select and selfish few.

This closed mindedness is what has led us to the precipice of disaster.

Not the war or civil unrest kind of disaster, but something that has more far reaching repercussions. Global warming does not discriminate based on geography, and there is not a corner of this planet that will not be devastated by the repercussions of climate change.

Beyond the pollution and toxicity that we pour into our environment, a vast number of people are also burdened by the denseness of heavy, low frequency emotions like hate, anger and fear.

Violence erupts easily in communities that used to be safe, and that violence breeds more violence as fear spreads like a plague.

In the United States our children cannot feel safe going to school anymore, and are reminded daily of threats to their safety by the presence of metal detectors and armed police officers in their schools. Their parents are reminded of the reality of gun violence by the perpetual onslaught of true stories of assaults and deaths on the news. And of course this constant threat of violence has repercussions on the short and long term mental health of those who have to live with it.

And the fears of physical harm that are so pervasive in our cultures breed more anger, violence and harm.

Disintegration of Community

It has not always been like this. As recently as four decades ago there was more love and compassion shared by neighbors. There was less fear of being out after dark, and more time spent with loved ones rather than chained to desks at jobs that are necessary for us to pay an ever growing pile of bills.

For our purposes, I will refer to community as a network rather than a geographic location. With our evolution into more of a global society, you may have friends and family around the world; and if they emotionally support you, or you them, they are considered to be part of your community.

Most people have some form of community; but as much of the world has modernized, we have forgotten how important it is to who we are.

It is not the long hours of work, geographic moves or the physical breaking apart of extended family structures that are to blame for any of this.

The disconnect was caused by our cultural obsession with money and material objects that society falsely claims will be a conduit for happiness and prestige.

And it is exacerbated by a predominant global focus on competition rather than cooperation and collaboration.

None of the money, possessions or focus on "winning" matters.

All that matters is love.

When we remember who we are meant to be, and we slow down to connect more with our communities, *it dissolves the hurt.*

The hurting is created by loneliness, while surrounded by people.

Isolation prevents humans from thriving. We are a tribal species and we feel whole when we are in connection with others who are loving and supportive to us and who we love and support.

Technology can help, but when left unchecked it hurts many by contributing to the feelings of isolation.

During the pandemic, technology helped large numbers of people work and stay connected; and it was considered to be an indispensable tool by them.

Technology & the Human Heart

But technology has been taken too far. Many have chosen to give into the addictive cravings of dopamine hits that come from a "like" or a gaming win, and they use technology in destructive ways.

Use of technology to deteriorate rather than build community has become pervasive, with couples and entire families keeping their noses in their phones for entertainment rather than spending time together making eye contact and conversation.

Phones "ping" and conversations are interrupted or completely aborted while one party scrambles to see what communication or news they may not want to miss.

Technology can assist with human connection over long distances when it is used intentionally to listen and communicate.

Scrolling and responding to pings, and allowing technology to interrupt our in-person interactions has taken over the first world and is a threat to our survival.

I know that sounds extreme so please stay open and consider the following:

Your time is one of your most precious resources and many people currently spend an exorbitant amount of time in mindless activities on their phones, computers or televisions.

There is nothing wrong with indulging in occasional entertainment, but what is it that this allocation of time takes away from?

1. It is likely to be lessening their time spent in connection and fellowship with others, and that connection is something everyone needs. Creating human connection is part of our instinctual programming; and having real connection, or community, is required for optimum mental health. It does not matter if you consider yourself to be a "people person" or whether you are an introvert or extrovert. We are a species that thrives in community with others.

Everyone thrives in community.

2. It is likely to be limiting time spent in pursuing more brain stimulating hobbies such as art, music, reading or writing. All of these activities can be pursued for entertainment, and have the benefit of adding to your brain's neuroplasticity in ways that scrolling, watching movies or playing video games will not.

The human brain is not meant to atrophy with age. This is a manifestation created by a lack of use of our mental facilities.

It is caused by people ceasing to expand their mind over their lifetime; and by too many in first world countries spending senseless hours in mindless endeavors.

3. When excessive time is spent in mindless pursuits, it contributes to depression, emotional eating and other mental disorders. It is easy and dangerous for people to become accustomed to the dopamine hit they get from these isolating online activities. They allow it to replace the similar hormonal stimulation that God intended us to seek, and which is received from connection, creativity and the pursuit of goals.

4. It has been proven that people in this modern age have less goals and productive pursuits than we or our predecessors did just twenty years ago. Often, this stems from filling in exorbitant amounts of time with technology in ways that are unproductive and excessively habit forming.

Many people in more "advanced" cultures on the planet have lost their connection with others.

Technology is an advantageous tool that will be instrumental in our continued advancements and evolution, but it can also be a detriment when it is not used with thoughtfulness and intentionality.

It is paramount to our survival as a species that we intentionally pursue more human interaction, looking to connect with love and an open heart in our communities.

And when hearts connect, the miraculous happens.

Moods lift and compassion reigns supreme, *and shared compassion dissolves the hurt.*

Change is inevitable. Wise leaders
anticipate it and adapt quickly.

The Challenges & Joys of Evolution

Our current quandary is nobody's fault. It is part of the challenge of evolution. It has been part of our evolutionary path all along, to make mistakes and learn from them.

But we have not yet accepted the challenge to evolve, by choosing to learn and improve from our modern mistakes.

We have not yet, as a global community, chosen to allow everyone to have their own experience.

We have not yet chosen to take the fork in the road that leads to what is good for the majority, rather than the one that leads to wealth for the few.

The Challenge of Consumerism

When barter is no longer the primary method of survival, it becomes possible to earn more currency. And that opens the door to new possibilities to acquire more things.

And "things" can then easily be misconstrued as a contributor to happiness, measurement of worth or a grounds for comparing ourselves to others.

Rationalizations to work harder abound. It may be a drive to work more so that they can buy a new and bigger car, even though the current car is fine.

Or an ambition to work more hours to stand out for a promotion, so that they can afford to take exotic vacations.

Or a desire to earn more so they can buy more stuff to contribute to their shopping addiction.

We are creative beings. It is part of our nature, programming and drive for fulfillment to have and seek to create goals.

Unfortunately for many in the developed parts of the world, their goals have become tied to money and material possessions; and all of those seemingly necessary, long working days often take them away from human connection.

And human connection fuels our soul.

When your grandparents were born (or perhaps your parents depending on their ages), the general population's goals and ways to fulfillment were simpler; and in first world countries, those who had their basic needs met were generally happier than the population today.

This is because people in our modern era are exhausted. They have lists to get through that are a mile long and many are required to work excessive hours just to make ends meet.

Being overburdened by work was not created by consumerism, however. We have had a spiraling out of control economy that has created a massive gap between the rich and everyone else. Many people struggle to maintain a roof over their heads and feed their families while working two jobs. At the same time, some have more excess funds than they can use and feel compelled by societal norms to buy "more things" like extra homes they only visit a few weeks a year.

Financial ecosystems are broken when the disparity is so vast; but more significant to current suffering is the fact that our connection to each other has broken down. Many of those with excess wealth feel a necessity to hoard it, rather than using it for the betterment of the human condition and uplifting those in need.

We are one human race and human community. ***And when our brothers and sisters are suffering, we all lose.***

There is nothing wrong with acquiring wealth or having

nice things. Our downward spiral started because of hoarding, greed and a constant *need* for more things.

Each and every conscious member of our first world nations will be well served to regularly review where their priorities are. It is an ongoing challenge and awareness we must build and perpetuate due to the culture of materialism that bombards us.

As an example, someone desiring a promotion that will mean more stress, responsibility and longer hours worked may be thinking that they should climb the corporate ladder for the benefit of what it allows them to give to their family. The question would be if their family really needs more money and the status that more things will provide, or would having more time to spend with them be more advantageous in the long run?

Everyone's situation is different and will change over time, requiring constant reevaluation and going back to the question - what is the true priority here?

When I was younger, I made the decision to stop my climb up the corporate ladder and stay in one job for an extended period. It meant less money and prestige over time, and was not the path I had envisioned when I was in college. But I enjoyed the benefits of a short commute and some flexibility in my schedule, which as a working mom of four I prioritized.

As my children were growing up, I would constantly reevaluate our continuously rising expenses against my stagnant income, and had to rethink our priorities regularly. A few of my decisions, such as not having cable television at home and driving an old paid off car until it became too expensive to fix, did not make me popular with my children. In fact, I am quite sure they thought of us as "poor". That term is all relative though. I had chosen to focus on other priorities such as a monthly contribution to their college funds.

Action item: Set aside some time to look at your hours of "work". If your work happens to be your soul's purpose, you may not see it as work or need to limit your time spent in that pursuit. This exercise is meant for those who feel pulled to work more than forty hours a week doing something that pays their bills but does not fuel them and bring them joy.*

Are you living to work or working to live? If your expenses are compelling you to work more than you would like, are there any you could give up or minimize? What regular expenses go beyond meeting your basic needs and are therefore optional?

You do not have to give anything up, but it is enlightening to regularly draw your attention to the extras and what you may be committing to or giving up elsewhere, such as more stress or time spent with loved ones. There is always a trade-off.

After reviewing this list, try to identify ways you might consider reducing your spending without feeling deprived. Sometimes it just requires questioning why we do what we do.

This exercise serves two purposes that are a priority throughout this narrative. The first would be to potentially create less financial need so that you may potentially work less, and free up some time to make a difference in other ways. I will elaborate on living your purpose later, and although it does not always necessitate a full-time commitment, there is always time involved.

Time is one of our greatest resources and something most first world inhabitants believe themselves to be short on; but this is a misperception. We each have plenty of time but what most people will benefit from is more effective priority setting.

The second benefit from this exercise will be to help you identify any potential excess in your current budget that you could relegate to a worthy cause. Not everyone has both time and money to contribute to improving the human condition, but most can find one or the other if challenged to do so.

* Regarding work that does not bring you joy - there are two ways to look at this. We spend too much of our lives working to be doing something that we do not enjoy. If your work is not enjoyable, you should:

   a)   Consider changing it. Are you really stuck, or are you allowing fear of the unknown to keep you there? Ninety-nine percent of the time, you are there by choice.

   b)   Choose to enjoy what you do. Again, every human has free choice. If you cannot find any other reason, find joy in your work because it yields a paycheck.

Recognize that both scenarios are choices and something that you can choose to change.

The Human Survival Instinct

When push comes to shove, most of our challenge and resistance to evolving can be attributed to mankind's survival instincts.

You may have experienced some of this instinctual programming as a hindrance in your life or noticed it as a detriment in the lives of others.

Have you ever observed someone coming to a conclusion and arguing a point before the other person is finished outlining theirs? Or perhaps you remember a time when you witnessed an accident or some kind of an emergency and most of the people around you stood frozen and stared like a deer stuck in the headlights. Or you may have been frustrated to witness a friend or family member going through a tough time and they did not take action to help change their circumstances.

We actually see examples like this everyday, without necessarily accounting for the cause.

We have many programs running in our subconscious that we are not aware of, and yet they impact our perspectives and behaviors. Those that are the hardest to circumvent, are the ones that have been with us since birth. These are the instincts that were originally intended to ensure humanity's survival and which are not as relevant to our modern existence. In fact in most instances, rather than ensuring our survival in the twenty-first century, they now limit our progress.

Our survival instincts are insidious in nature, and the first necessary step for being able to work past them is an awareness that they are there.

We have the instinct to cling to what is familiar.

This is also referred to in modern vernacular as staying in our comfort zone. This instinct habituated from a learned behavior of hiding in caves where primitive humans could be protected from both the elements and the possible danger of wild animals. We learned that the cave, or staying within the confines of what was familiar, was safe; and anyone who ventured out further than usual to explore or seek food, quite often never returned. It was presumed they met their doom and that it was safer to stay where it was familiar.

We have an instinctual fear of new things, people or circumstances.

Because of our instinct to stay with what is familiar, these things are interpreted by our brain as a possible threat or danger, which creates fear at a subconscious and often unrecognized level. This instinctual fear creates the fight - flight - or freeze reaction which is our evolutionary learned response to combat danger. Which response we activate is determined by the situation and strengths of the individual. As an example, if the danger is an immediate physical threat to someone who considers themselves to be stronger than they are fast, they will plant their feet, hold their ground and prepare to fight. Someone who is fleet on their feet will run and someone who considers themselves to be neither will "freeze" or attempt to hide from the threat.

You may have noticed this at play in your own life. When confronted with a new scenario or opportunity, you may not recognize fear but notice being overwhelmed with indecision or an inability to move forward, which is the freeze response. Or you might experience an irrational pull in a different direction which distracts you and would be a flight response. Or you could feel an out of proportion need to justify or defend what you are currently doing rather than consider a different option; and that would be a fight response.

In all of these examples, the resistance is created by your subconscious to keep you safe; and staying safe is interpreted by your subconscious as staying in familiar circumstances.

We have an instinct to "fight" for ourselves and our family.

This was a stronger and more relevant instinct when we were cavemen, but you can still recognize this reaction today when people fight to be right in their beliefs, and they are unwilling to listen to opposing viewpoints.

It is not just their insular way of thinking. It is an instinct to stick with what they know and to protect what they believe they know to be true, in order for their family to benefit from it as well.

As an example, someone going to war for their freedom or a particular religious or political ideology is not just volunteering to die for something they believe in. Frequently they are martyring themselves to protect that ideology for their family as well. They are, quite literally in this instance, fighting to hold onto an existing or future vision of a particular circumstance or ideology.

Another instinct that drives some humans is an evolutionary instinct to mate.

This has led to some dysfunctional outcomes.

In many cultures we now have an incessant pressure and deadline put forward to procreate. This includes a societal expectation to be with a partner of the opposite sex by a certain age, for the ultimate goal of having children.

The instinct was originally instilled in humans to ensure the survival of the species; but with over eight billion people on the planet at the time of this writing, it's well past time to take the pressure off the younger generation to meet this expectation of many societies. It is well past time to allow them to be happy, in whatever manner that means for them, as they pursue their life's path and purpose.

No one *needs* a partner or children to be happy or to be fulfilled in living their purpose.

In reality, there are more people on earth right now who do not have children as part of their life's path, than those who do.

And as a side note, currently in most cultures around the globe, the likelihood of being happy as a single person is greater than if you marry. This is because many succumb to pressure and end up in a mismatch which they then stay in, also due to pressure from their finances, culture or belief systems.

This cultural expectation is fueled by our patriarchal systems and goes hand in hand with the continued subjugation of women as the weaker and less worthy gender. It is convenient for these patriarchies to reinforce this cultural narrative in order to minimize the threat they feel from strong women.

We also have the instinct to hoard.

It is an innate instinct to save food or other necessities, to get us through a barren off-season or a drought. Throughout human evolution, there were times when this instinct served us well.

Some reading this may be old enough to remember stories from your parents or grandparents living through the Great Depression or the subsequent world war. Supplies of many essentials continued to be short after the depression because resources were all channeled to war efforts. The generations that lived through those sparse times had this hoarding instinct reinforced through their circumstances, and then taught their children to be frugal and hoard. They taught their families to save money, food or other necessities for the unexpected "rainy day".

All of these instincts are past the point of usefulness at this juncture in our evolution, but continue to play out to varying degrees in most people's lives.

Yes, even the instinct of hoarding is no longer relevant with our global society, and it has significantly contributed to the predominance of suffering around the planet. It is wise to be good stewards of our money and other possessions and to purchase or discard them with discernment, but a hoarding mentality is harmful to our greater good.

There are plenty of resources available. It is an abundant planet.

It is the hoarding instinct, and the subsequent greed that stems from it, that has led to suffering for so many under-resourced people on the planet.

It is those who have a majority of the world's wealth and continue to amass great wealth and other resources, who have perpetuated the suffering by turning a blind eye to it. The suffering around the planet has expanded rather than lessening as it could, because of the many who continue to greedily accumulate resources without concern for others.

Overriding Instinctual Programming

*Instincts are automatic behaviors **that we allow.***

> *We each have the power of free choice, and therefore we can choose different behaviors.*

This isn't hyperbole. This is how humans are meant to develop throughout their lives.

You may have heard the expression that we are made in God's image. What this means is that just like our creator, we are creative beings and are meant to always be seeking to expand - both ourselves and our circumstances.

This is not counterintuitive to eliminating greed or a need to hoard. When you are constantly expanding your circumstances, it is easier to move beyond a lack and hoarding mindset.

We are meant to have goals and to continuously be learning and improving ourselves and our creations.

The first step to circumventing our instinctive programs and limiting paradigms, is to build an awareness that they are impacting our lives most of the time. By reading this explanation of humanity's inherent instincts that impede both our progress and ultimate happiness, you have created your own awareness.

Once you are aware, you can become intentional in looking for how any of these behaviors show up in your life. Without judgment, watch for and evaluate which instincts are most problematic and in what situations they come up for you.

Once you have recognized an unhelpful behavior such as fighting for your beliefs rather than seeking a middle ground or consensus, you can take a brief pause and *choose a different behavior.*

In this instance you might choose to ask some thoughtful questions of the person holding the opposing viewpoint, with the goal of understanding that viewpoint. You do not need to hold the same beliefs in order to develop an understanding of why they hold theirs.

And this understanding will lead to compassion.

Compassion is the underlying attribute necessary for all consensus building and peace.

It will help you navigate every relationship or circumstance that involves other people.

You can choose to move past fear that keeps you in your comfort zone.

You can choose to allow new information into your awareness and seek resolutions when there is conflict.

You can choose to embrace new behaviors when there is a compelling argument for the greater good of all.

You can choose to evolve past all of the instincts that we no longer need for our survival.

Exercise:

Take some quiet time to think into the following prompts and record your responses.

Where could you have resistance of any type showing up in your life?

We all have it and it can take many forms. Brainstorm the

numerous ways you can hold yourself or others back. Things to look out for include:

1. Showing up late or completely missing appointments that may lead to some type of opportunity or change.

2. Resisting listening to other people's viewpoints. Having an incessant urge to argue or convince them of yours.

3. An overwhelming desire to be liked or approved of. This may not be recognized but can show up as holding yourself back or not speaking up when you have a different opinion or viewpoint.

4. Confusion, indecision or analysis paralysis which leads to delaying any change or contemplated action.

Write everything down that comes to mind, and then review your list and determine which one area is the biggest drawback for you right now. You cannot change or work past everything at once, so pick one obstacle that you would like to work through first.

Next, knowing what you now know about human instincts, think about why this resistance is coming up.

Your subconscious never works against you. It just wants to keep you safe.

When you recognize what the true underlying fear is, you can determine if it is valid or not.

Is there a reasonable threat to your survival or just a misinterpretation of what a potential change or new perspective could mean to you?

In most instances, even when there is some type of risk, it is outweighed by the benefits. Do your due diligence and analyze the pros and cons. Once you have done this, and you have determined that it is wise to move through the resistance, you now have fodder to feed your subconscious.

Next you will want to tell it what you found. Reason with it. Your subconscious is part of you and very smart. When you point out the facts of your risk analysis, it will understand and lessen or completely release the resistance.

This is a really powerful exercise to do anytime you are challenged to move forward. Do not be shy about having this conversation with yourself.

In order to effectively communicate with the subconscious, you must speak your argument out loud and then repeat it silently to yourself; and sometimes you will need to repeat it in different words, over the course of a few days. You will want to enumerate your argument both silently and out loud because your subconscious hears your spoken words differently than your thoughts, and the combination of both is the most all encompassing path to piercing through the resistance quickly.

Repeat this exercise anytime you feel like you are holding yourself back, and continue repeating your risk analysis to your subconscious each day until you feel the resistance dissipate and you are able to take your first small action.

The Upside of Evolution

It is not all bad of course. Modernization has many benefits that can in fact contribute to our emotional health and overall well being.

Travesties can be circumvented by sharing our passion and advocacy online.

Families can connect online when they are separated geographically.

Inventions exist that are making our lives easier, longer and healthier.

When circumstances require swift action, communication technology makes it possible to implement.

Science has advanced to the point that we know we are all energy. This has opened the door to more acceptance of energy healing, which is changing the trajectory of health practices.

We know more about the harmful effects of toxins in our environment, food and pharmaceuticals so that people are able to make wiser choices, improving their longevity.

Where does this all lead?

Our resources are vast and new knowledge is gained by the minute, but greed and corruption are turning our world into an abomination of toxic ruin.

This is the challenge of evolution.

With expanding knowledge comes greater responsibility, and our world has not yet stepped up to meet this obligation.

As conscious world citizens, we have a responsibility to protect the planet and human life first.

And to develop advancements to make lives better as we can, secondarily.

This may sound intuitive, but it is important to highlight at this juncture because many of the advancements we have made that look like progress, are killing our planet.

It is a dangerous circumstance and frequent occurrence when industry leaders are allowed to push their discoveries and advancements forward without thoughtful and thorough vetting.

Depending on the scope and complexity of the project, this could involve years of research, enlisting computer modeling to project possibilities and potential pitfalls. It should also involve small group beta testing as so-called advancements with far reaching implications are rolled out cautiously.

It is not the consumer who is pushing the quick proliferation of technological advancements into the market. It is the companies who are focused on the extensive cost of research and beta testing, versus their potential for creating immediate profits. And it is our governments who are failing their citizens by allowing the companies to do it.

When left to their own decision making, companies that lack ethical leadership will continue to make decisions in favor of profitability rather than caution and the best interests of humanity.

Going back to our long forgotten heritage of honoring Mother Earth and all of her creatures is the only possible solution.

It is the only way we will continue to survive.

Peace will be ours when love
supersedes the need to be right.

Proliferating Peace

Millennia of conflict does not define us.

Throughout our recorded history there have been wars, usually in the name of a religion or resources that create wealth.

It is painful to acknowledge that human lives have been wasted due to greed, throughout time. Often this is coupled with a presumptuous belief that only they know the truth or best path and those who do not accept it should die.

Perusing humanity's long written history, you will be hard pressed to find a war, ever, that makes sense.

And yet we have the ability to value human life and behave better. We have been given the ability to choose our thoughts and behaviors. We have free choice to override our instincts and other self-sabotaging programming.

Nothing on earth is as precious as human life, and yet it as been taken so lightly throughout time. It is mind numbing to think about.

All of the wars and death are not entirely mankind's fault, however. We are each a product of our fears and societal programming. If you are brought up with the belief that killing can be justified, then of course you will see nothing wrong with it.

Shifting the Paradigm

Accepting war as an option is a perspective and perspectives can shift. Our history of conflict and violence does not have to define our future, unless we allow it to.

Humans are in fact very resilient and malleable. We have survived an abundance of adversity throughout history and we are still here to tackle the next obstacle. Along with our survival instincts, we have an innate ability to change and adapt with our circumstances.

We have the ability to create a new paradigm of peace. What we currently lack, is the DESIRE.

If we want to survive, we must create a world where love defines all of our interactions.

We are at a tipping point and have the opportunity to create a new era where human life is valued over gold or other resources.
The new era we create together will be a time when we have compassion for others and everyone is accepted and loved ***despite any real or perceived differences.***

This better world will be a place where it is OK and even encouraged to be different, because the uniqueness that each of us holds is our superpower. It is part of how we were created and are meant to contribute to the world.

Our commonalities will bond us,
because we are one human race.

And our differences will continue to make us special and will make innovation and societal betterment possible.

When we are able to honor the beliefs and differing perspectives presented by others as a contribution to our problem solving and evolutionary growth, our world can shift its current paradigm of accepted violence.

How boring our world would be if everyone always agreed, looked and thought just alike. Differences are the path to improvements. Each person has their perspective on a particular topic, which is just one in a myriad of possibilities.

If everyone shared the same perspective, we would limit our ability to problem solve as humans.

And this one shift *from differences being a problem to being an opportunity,* allows peaceful dialogue, new ideas and innovations **and is the short leap we need to make in order to proliferate peace in the world.**

This is the power of the mastermind that we must enable and embrace.

Our world is full of brilliant minds that are being guided with divine inspiration, and those ideas need an outlet. We do not need to adopt all of their ideas. That would be unwise because not all inspired ideas are meant to be fully produced. Some are meant to guide us into conversations and additional ideation.

But the first step is to be open to outside of the box, new or different ideas and perspectives.

We must be willing to listen, not for the purpose of arguing our point, but with the intention to fully hear and understand the full spectrum of new possibilities. And productive dialogue is just the first step.

The second will be allowing love and compassion to pave the best path forward.

When everyone has the greatest good of humanity at heart rather than personal or national gains, everything can be resolved by thoughtful contemplation, dialogue and the initiation of best practices that support the majority.

Our diversity is what defines us as individuals and *leveraging those differences will help us to rebuild the planet.*

Peace is Profitable

"Industry first" as a mantra has taken over our first world culture. So allow me to make this make sense for the corporate money makers who appear to need to support any proposition put forward. This enables us to reduce a majority of the current resistance to peace proposals because many believe that peace must also be good for profit.

And peace *is* profitable.

Economies thrive in times of peace. Besides the obvious and insidious cost of human life, a war effort channels vast quantities of a nation's money and resources to the war machine, including guns and other killing apparatus.

When a country is at peace and insulated from rumblings of a coming conflict, its people can look beyond an immediate threat. They spend more and are more willing to try new things. This freedom from the bombardment of threats which cause fear and emotional upheaval, allows for more comfort and frees individual spending patterns.

Everyone spends more when
they are more relaxed and happy.

Peace is also good for industry because more innovation happens in times of peace.

And innovation leads to businesses standing out, growing and thriving.

The ability to turn lackluster corporate performance into a gold mine comes with innovation. And innovation is a very risky business during a war.

Have you ever noticed a song that gets a lot of air time on the radio? It may be your type of music, but when it is overplayed, your enthusiasm wanes. You become bored with the same old song and change the channel.

This is what happens with consumers in war time. They get tired of being asked to channel resources to the war effort, and they stop paying attention. It does not matter what someone is selling at that point, the potential consumers are not listening. They are tired, scared and distracted.

When peace is the norm, their ears open and the audience for those goods and services broadens. There is nothing like peace to lull customers back into spending mode.

Peace and innovation are the precursors for a thriving economy.

Then there are the financial costs of war itself. Where is that money being redirected from? Who or what is no longer being served?

There is a great monetary cost to war, and that money has to come from somewhere. Corporate taxes, perhaps? Or an uptick in fines to help the government raise money?

It does not matter what side you are on, or if your country is actively engaged in war or channeling resources to one that is, **everyone loses.** Including the giants of industry.

Peace through Unconditional Love

As mentioned previously, love is the very fabric of the universe, because God is love and in all things. Love is who we are, and embracing it is the only way for your soul to thrive.

When we discover and nurture unconditional love for all of our fellow humans, conflict recedes.

In most of the world's cultures, we have actually been conditioned to fight so it is no surprise that conflict proliferates.

From the time anyone can remember, we have been taught to compete and try to best others. And when we do not win or get our way, it is devastating. You may even perceive a loss of parental approval or a reward you were looking forward to.

We are taught that it is a cut throat world and that we must compete and come out on top, to the detriment of the "losers". What a concept.

We are taught to equate subjugating others to a desired experience such as praise from a parent or authority figure.

And so many of us have learned to compete, and not to value collaboration or compromise.

Compromise is not winning, and that equates to losing; and losing is not something we can tolerate. *It is for losers.*

Collaborating and working on solutions in community and cooperation with others, rather than competition and one-upmanship, is the only way to create a thriving and peaceful society.

And a culture of collaboration needs to start at home. If the home consists of more than one adult, they should be working in collaboration for the family, rather than one partner dominating and the other acquiescing. This may sound like an obvious relationship dynamic to aspire to create, but in many societies this type of collaborative partnership is not taught or welcomed. There is a dominant person, usually determined by age or gender, that often takes on the role of dictator in the household: and they create an environment lacking in open dialogue and cooperation among all of the family members. When children grow up in an environment like this, they are programmed to expect it as a requirement for societal functioning.

This type of open communication and collaboration that is necessary for a changed and peaceful world, will also need to be taught in schools. The majority of formal educational structures around the globe are dysfunctional and in need of complete restructuring. Schools must prioritize the teaching and modeling of attributes such as curiosity, listening and sharing of creative ideas. They must also encourage cooperative projects and play. This new model would replace the current practices that reinforce individual scholastic accomplishment and sports competitions as the ideal.

A focus on collaboration rather than individual accomplishment is a foundational precept of any future society that engenders peace.

So how do individuals change the current tide of global hate and aggression? For most of us who are unable to influence world politics, it must start with managing ourselves and our daily interactions.

When we manage our emotions, it becomes easier to share love and compassion.[9]

And when we encourage respectful dialogue and collaboration in all of our relationships and interactions, we each do our part in starting a ripple that others will be inspired to emulate.

Identities that Don't Serve Humanity

Your identity defines who you are and how you act. It is based in your subconscious so there are parts of it you may not be consciously aware of, but there are also many elements you will recognize. Often the way we consciously identify is based on circumstances that are out of our control and have no relevance to what our identity actually is.

Frequently we identify ourselves by our culture, national ties, gender, familial status, roles, religion and ethnicity; and there are current trends to promote and glorify these ties to external things as an identity.

But none of these are who you are at a subconscious identity level.

And these circumstantially based identity assumptions are what has proliferated the divisions that are the foundation of all wars and conflict.

It is what keeps people living busy but unfulfilled lives. The association with those circumstances that are not who they really are, keeps them in their roles defined by society rather than following their soul's path.

Identity has nothing to do with any of this. It is how you see yourself interacting in the world. It is who you feel capable of being. It is often dictated by our past and therefore your interpretation of your identity is rarely accurate, and this can hold your back from your true potential.

Your identity does not have anything to do with your background and paradigms however. It is connected to your self-love and esteem.

And who you are at your core identity, is God's love and light.

You are here to love and serve others. You are an imperfect human who is on their journey, learning and evolving throughout your life. And you are part of one global, human race.

We are all the same.

We are ALL God's creation. We each have divinity within us. And we are all imperfect, with the opportunity to choose to improve ourselves every day of our lives.

There is no being better or less than anyone else when we are all God's creation.

It does not matter if you have a higher IQ or more physical beauty. It does not matter what country you reside in or what your ethnicity or skin color is… or your gender or sexual identity… or your religious beliefs.

 God loves each of us the same and unconditionally.

It does not matter if you have made some horrific mistakes in your life and have not tried to "repent" or atone for your sins. God loves you and will continue to attempt to communicate with you regarding better choices in the future.

And they will still love you if you do not hear that communication, or choose not to follow it.

This begs the question - If we are all God's creation and equal in their eyes, what gives any of us the right to take another person's life? Whether it is war or legal justifications for the death penalty, life and death are not meant to be decided by other people.*

Identifying with outside circumstances is what has caused most wars. National borders and religious beliefs create boundaries and divisions that seem irreconcilable. And yet, if those assumptive identities were removed, there would be nothing for those groups to fight about. There would be no tribal bonding around one distinct belief being right. We would allow individuals to reach their own understandings and have their own experiences.

Identity is not circumstantial or immutable.

It is meant to uplevel over our lifetime and support us in who we were *created to be, before all of the labels and self imposed limits.*

As each person honors and allows everyone else to have their unique experience of life, they will let go of attachment to controlling what others do, believe or align themselves with. And our world can rest.

Earth will be at peace.

* I feel the need to clarify this statement as it applies to the concepts of abortion and suicide. This statement is not meant as justification for the "pro-life" or anti assisted death arguments. No one makes these decisions lightly and governments should not be involved, or inflict the beliefs of those in power onto anyone making these very personal decisions. I encourage everyone to seek guidance from their inner wisdom. Each individual's

circumstances and path will be unique and should be honored.

With a surge in the acceptance of energy healing as we navigate into a new era of understanding, mental health issues and suicide rates will decline. The vast majority are caused by trapped emotions, and are easily resolved when people are open to energy healing.

Sincere appreciation for what we have,
is the first step toward preventing its loss.

Protecting Our Planet

This is a book of hope; but one can not have hope for a better future without recognizing the failings of the present and being willing to seek the change necessary to create that better time.

To be really succinct in outlining our current predicament...

> *We are on the precipice of total annihilation of life on our planet.*

There is no time left to mince words.

We are destroying our planet through the complete disregard for its delicate balance that our modern advancements and indulgences are decimating.

There is a way forward; but first allow me to reflect on the present state of toxic anarchy that our myopic devotion to over indulgence and commercialism has created.

How Our Planet Rolls

Earth is a macrocosm of many ecosystems. Each is meant to work together harmoniously, to ensure the survival of all.

The atmosphere, oceans, forests, plains and mountains all encompass ecosystems that ensure earth's survival. When one system breaks down, it's like a house of cards falling. *They will all fail.*

It is like a beautiful symphony where each instrument has an important role to play. If one section gets off key or their timing is out of sync, the song will be ruined.

We are at a tipping point with the delicate balance between and amongst all of the ecosystems on our planet right now.

The rising carbon emissions in our atmosphere are causing the ocean and atmospheric temperatures all around the planet to rise at an alarming rate. In 2024, the average land and ocean surface temperature was 2.32 degrees Fahrenheit above the 20th century average.[10] A rise of this magnitude has never been observed before, and has significant global ramifications.

The higher water surface temperatures and change in ocean currents this brought about, are causing unprecedented rainfall and flooding, as well as drought and an increase in forest fires. The excessively high temperature of tropic waters is causing the death of algae and coral reefs which are both significant to the water ecosystems.

The increase of carbon dioxide in our oceans has led to rising acidification, reducing the PH of the ocean by thirty percent since the preindustrial era.[11] All of these potentially deadly changes cause a ripple effect through every level of the marine ecosystems and beyond. As various species approach extinction from the severity of these stressors, the ripple it causes has far reaching implications. When one ecosystem struggles, they all begin to fail.

Another tragic and terminal circumstance is the rampant deforestation both from unchecked development and raging wildfires. These will only become more frequent and far reaching with the climbing temperatures and unprecedentedly high winds. Beyond the obvious and immediate tragedies from the wildfires, the loss of so many trees is dramatically adding to the atmosphere's increasing CO_2 levels. As you may remember from science class, trees help remove carbon dioxide from our air through photosynthesis, and produce oxygen in return. Deforestation and wildfires reduce the number of trees on the planet to process CO_2 and contribute oxygen to our air; and when the trees are cut down or burned, the stored carbon dioxide in the tree, roots and surrounding soil are released into the air.

Over time as oxygen levels are reduced in our atmosphere, our lungs will have to work harder to obtain the oxygen that our bodies need to function optimally. The long term impact of this is unknown, but since our bodies are miraculous ecosystems of their own, we can logically infer that it will have a negative impact that will worsen as the oxygen in our air continues to decrease.

In the end, whether it's dying toxic oceans or a loss of forests that lead to air we can't breathe and oceans that can't support the inhabitants, the end result is the same.

In any of these continuing scenarios we all lose.

All of these circumstances currently exist and we, the people of this beautiful planet, are running out of time to "fix" the intensifying destruction mankind has wrecked.

There have been too many years of arguing about the existence of climate change, precipitated by financial concerns and a desire to avoid personal inconvenience.

And yet none of it will matter if we are left with a planet that no one and nothing can survive on.

It sounds like a science fiction movie.

But sadly, it is not.

It is a reality we are creating right now by uncaring actions that destroy rather than care for our planet.

In the past, it was the custom of landowners to care for their land so that it stayed healthy and could be passed on to another generation. But as more and more people left the land to find work in office buildings or online, we have slowly forgotten our connection to Mother Earth.

We have forgotten her importance and significance in our lives. We have lost the respect and love that our ancestors gave her, and we are allowing uncaring corporate greed to kill her.

The planet is our responsibility for just a short time during the course of our lives. Life on the planet in its various forms has been here for eons; but if we do not care for it like we want life to continue for future generations, it may not be here for our personal futures either.

With the current trajectory of rising temperatures and acidification of our oceans, we are on course for the oceans to be dead from the culmination of stressors in just five years. This extrapolates into a dead toxic planet.

Delicate ecosystems that have to stay healthy and support each other is how our planet rolls.

> *Each ecosystem must work together in*
> *harmony and in support of the whole.*

Of course we are talking about humanity in this narrative, but humanity cannot survive in a bubble and must live in harmony with the rest of God's creations on this planet.

The Greenhouse Catastrophe

There is a lot of denial around global warming and the greenhouse effect, but the fact that temperatures are rising and weather patterns are becoming more severe and unpredictable cannot be denied.

It is a reality whose repercussions can be observed around the globe. And yet its denial is prevalent. It does not matter what someone's ideology or national affiliation is. It also is not related to socioeconomic status or a host of other variables we could compare. In every country around the globe where people are advanced enough to follow world news, there is discussion and the subsequent denial of climate change.

We have all seen political campaigns run on the premise that it does not exist. We have been told that it will hurt the economy, or elicit some other claimed repercussions if action is taken to eliminate it.

We have heard world leaders espouse the need for changes and then back pedal and leave everything the same, or worse than when they started.

We have seen the repercussions of subterfuge that cultivate a proliferation of criticism of the science and research involved. We have seen a total disregard from those in authority, for the real life pain and destruction, as well as economic repercussions that the effects of climate change are eliciting around the globe.

We know the impact it is having and continue to be flummoxed by the lack of leaders in pivotal positions who **should be willing to stand up for what is right and save the planet.**

Climate change is not a made-up notion for political gain or a reason for religious indignation. It really does not matter what anyone thinks is causing the changes that are currently pummeling the planet. They are real and will continue to worsen until we turn the tide on global warming.

What matters are the facts, so let's review a few:

1. The average temperature of the earth has risen dramatically. 2024 was the warmest year on record, with the land and ocean surface temperature exceeding the 20th century average by 2.32 degrees Fahrenheit, or 1.29 degrees Celsius.[13]

2. The global sea surface temperature reached an all time high in 2024, breaking records for the second year in a row.[14]

3. In many parts of the world, the water temperature hovers at or above 100 degrees Fahrenheit which is causing the death of coral reefs, algae and many creatures that rely on these ecosystems for sustenance or as a breeding habitat.[15]

4. As entire species disappear from our oceans, the oceans are becoming more acidic, which creates more toxicity. The acidification is amplified by the rising levels of CO_2 in the water. This toxic water continues as part of the global water cycle and becomes acid rain.

5. Higher temperatures and excessive wind patterns are devastating the earth's forests. As our trees continue to be depleted through deforestation and wildfires, the repercussions amplify. We are losing an excessive number of animals to extinction and the environmental impact is far reaching.[16]

6. Scientists have not determined the health impact of a

depletion of oxygen in the air we breathe, but we know that the human body is its own delicate ecosystem. Therefore it can be deduced that receiving less of the elements the body requires to thrive will have a significant long term impact on human health.

Each miraculous in its own right, the planet's ecosystems are interwoven and dependent on one another. When one microsystem endures a hardship, there is a ripple of disruption and imbalance throughout the others.

As an example, a tortoise is an unpretentious reptile that appears to have little value to add to society. But it is the sloughed dead skin from the tortoise's regular shedding that nourishes the dirt in their environments and creates more fertile soil. If all tortoises were to be removed or become extinct in a particular region, the repercussions would be vast.

Because plants adapt to their environment, those benefiting from the enriched soil would have come to require it and subsequently perish with the excess nourishment.

In turn, losing those plant varieties will impact the foraging habits of the other animals in that environment and lead to the malnutrition and eventual extinction of some of them. And so it goes. The cycle of depletion soon spirals out of control.

The current destruction from the planet's weather patterns cannot continue to be ignored. They will continue to create obvious devastation as well as ripples of unseen consequences, until humans become accountable for their actions; and we take major steps to change our current trajectory to extinction.

Time does not heal all things.
Sometimes action is necessary.

Earth Stewardship

The concept of stewardship almost seems too simple.

And it is simple, but not easy to implement given the current political divisiveness and financial repercussions.

The earth is currently a macrocosm of irresponsibility that has spiraled out of control over the past half of a century. Governments empower corporate greed, allowing pollution to proliferate instead of prioritizing clean air, water, and the protection of natural habitats for the numerous species that are quickly moving toward extinction.

Truncated efforts to save the environment abound, always minimized or stymied by money and the need to make more of it, regardless of the consequences.

Responsible action to protect our

**environment is not convenient or inexpensive,
which is why it is resisted.**

Added to this is the conundrum that humans at a core instinctual level are programmed to resist change.

Even when that change is good for us, our instinctual programming creates resistance.

Consequently, although the deadly spiral of climate change has been destroying the planet for several decades, the majority of the world's population has chosen to ignore the action necessary to stop this decimation of our environment. At one time, those necessary changes would have been minor; but given our current circumstances and lack of time to react, the adjustments to lifestyle and habits that will be necessary to create and sustain a turnaround are more dramatic.

A conversation about actions that require such a monumental effort by humanity, necessitates a review of the desired outcomes along with the inevitable consequences of continued inaction.

Upon reflection, most able thinking adults will agree that almost any intervention will be worth taking if it will lead to preserving our existence as a species.

This is *no longer a conversation about future generations.*

There are many self centered individuals who have chosen to not care about the future and have focused on their short term gains. But now everyone must focus on our current plight and how to save those of us who are here on earth right now.

The planet is on a crash course toward looming disaster. We are experiencing a foreshadowing of this through the current uptick in devastating and extreme weather events. The theoretical future of humanity will not matter if we cannot slow the pace of environmental destruction and **save our current population as we head toward extinction.**

Hope for a Healthy Planet

Around the globe, people have noticed an uptick in cataclysmic weather events. It seems to have built to a crescendo over the past 20 years, with many fearing where it will lead.

When will all of the heart wrenchingly bad news stop and how can we save ourselves from this continuous onslaught of fear-inducing events and chaos?

To be clear, I acknowledge that change is never easy. Deciding to orchestrate significant modifications to any regulations, processes or behaviors should never be taken lightly. It is always challenging to elicit buy in and orchestrate substantive change.

But we must change if we want to survive.

Our current trajectory toward destruction has us on track to extinct ourselves within the next five years.[17]

I am aware that this will sound like an unbelievable claim, until you take into account what your eyes can see in our current reality.

The scientific model that the world has referenced for the past 30 years, predicted harsh consequences if we do not improve our environmental stewardship and habits by 2050. This model has not been adapted, however, to keep pace with the quickly escalating temperatures and harsh weather patterns of the present.

If the model were to be adapted based on current data, the accelerating trajectory would catapult us into extinction by 2030. The Greenhouse Effect is now acting like a snowball speeding downhill. It has picked-up speed and scope, and is worsening at an alarming rate that was not predicted.

This is not hyperbole or rash extremism. And the downside of continuing to keep our heads in the sand and pretend that the planet is not in jeopardy, is the destruction of all life on the planet.

On the other hand, the only consequence of taking action quickly to protect the planet would be minor inconvenience and the ability to breathe more easily within a few years. This is as opposed to waiting decades for the existing tepid, environmentally friendly plans to come to fruition and prove themselves ineffective.

It does not seem like a hard choice does it?

And yet humanity waffles and waits for an easy solution to pop-up and save the planet.

Or for God to intervene and rescue us.

*The problem with asking God to save us is that we are **meant to co-create this next phase** of evolution by taking responsibility for our actions and stewarding our planet with love.*

If a beautiful new and toxin free environment were handed to us, our current behaviors would wreck it in short order. There is a saying that "God helps those who help themselves" and it applies in this scenario.

Everything in the universe operates through universal law, and if we want to manifest a beautiful planet that future generations will enjoy, we must take aligned action to create it now.

This means being responsible citizens of the earth as well as advocates for all life on the planet. In other words…

A new, golden era for humanity will arrive, *only after we take responsibility and action to create the environment we want to live in.*

The Aligned Actions Required

There is a lot of talk among those who care for the environment, about recycling and reducing your carbon footprint. These actions are important to your identity as a responsible earth steward and should be actualized by each of us to the best of our abilities. But these actions are a drop in the bucket compared to the massive shifts required to reduce carbon emissions and expedite an end to global warming.

And they are diluting our focus, distracting us from the truly culpable villains who are perpetuating this crisis.

The largest contributors to the planet's environmental problems are not individuals, but industries.

Sadly those industries have a powerful combination of clout. It includes both financial clout with governments and the clout of convenience offered to individuals. Subsequently they have not been reigned in as required to reverse our trajectory.

The energy production and transportation industries are by far the biggest contributors to the carbon emissions crisis. Because of their significant carbon imprint, it would be logical to think that these industries would have been required to go green by this juncture. And yet, very little progress has been made with alternative fuel sources and planet friendly transportation since the alarm was first sounded four decades ago.

One would think that significant progress would have been made, or that these would be the first areas to be regulated or ostensibly shut down. Unfortunately, any modifications to the energy and transportation industries will not only inconvenience everyone who relies on them, but will have financial repercussions throughout the world.

These are just two examples of impactful industries; and

between the service and supply interruptions and the jobs impacted, you can imagine the ripple of upset that regulating or scaling back any aspect of these industries will have. And yet it is an unavoidable conclusion that big changes in our habits and use of fossil fuels must happen.

When COVID-19 was at its peak in 2020 and the world seemed to shut down due to quarantine restrictions, the positive impact that this situation had on the environment was almost immediate. Within a month of the travel reductions, positive improvements were being measured across many environmental metrics.

The earth breathed a sigh of relief as humanity gave it a much needed break.

The gains were short lived however, and as soon as the quarantine was lifted and we were back to business as usual, the deterioration of our environment continued.

The actions now required to save the planet will be uncomfortable.

It will require progressive leaders from outside of the broken systems currently running our governments to advocate for the comprehensive restructuring and rebuilding needed. There must be many new systems developed that benefit the environment and will subsequently save us from extinction.

In the following chapters, we will explore the importance of a new type of leadership in moving us through these turbulent times. I invite you to stay open to your role.

Nothing is written in stone, but as you learn to recognize, trust and take action on your divine inspiration, you will notice your influence and impact widening. You just need to stay open to new possibilities.

A bridge is a path to new understanding.
Where you see anger, conflict or disagreement,
be a bridge.

Conscious Leadership & Purpose

When humanity finally understands that there is no other way forward and we must take action to save ourselves, *we will be able to transform our planet in quick order.*

That does not mean we will go back to our old and decadent ways once things have gotten better, however.

We cannot go back. There is no future for us in those old ways.

But we can create new ways.

New technologies and habits that benefit humanity will be developed to allow us to live in harmony with nature and each other. It will not happen overnight, but we are an innovative and resilient species.

Throughout history, when there was a need, humans

created a resulting product or service to meet it. This time will be no different.

When the ancient civilization of Crete was young, they developed processes that relied on the youth in unhealthy ways. As a society, they expected their younger members to work like pack mules whenever things needed to be hauled, which was daily. These excessive physical demands created a generation of crippled and arthritic men and women by the time they hit the ripe old age of thirty.

Everyone knew these practices were unsustainable and through a little divine inspiration, the wheel was invented. Before long there were more uses and adaptations to lighten their load and add convenience to their lives.

If you wonder why they were not given the idea a couple of generations sooner, the need or question has to be realized before inspired ideas materialize. If there is no need, no one looks for a solution.

We only get answers to the questions we ask.

Solutions will not become evident until a need is realized.

What did we see happen with the industrial revolution? There was a need to develop systems to support the growth of a new industry. Those systems evolved to include rules that mandated against the use of child labor. Labor law grew as a field to protect the rights of workers who were being abused. Unions were born from the need to advocate for groups who were being underserved. The entire field of labor morphed because there were needs. If industry had not created the need, those systems and regulations would not have materialized.

Divinity is standing ready to assist us through this pivotal time for humanity; but first we need to explore our vision and realize our needs.

Then we have to ask for guidance and listen.

Unnecessary habits may disappear, but those old ways that served a need will find new products or strategies to enable their survival.

In the near future, everyone must embrace the truth that our current way of life does not need to survive. It is not serving humanity. It must therefore be released, so that a new and more aligned and holistic way of life can be embraced.

We have developed self-perpetuating, destructive habits that cause poor health and other disastrous outcomes.

It is time for humanity to evolve; but in order to do so, our systems, structures and unhealthy habits need to evolve as well.

Our time of resistance must end. By being open to the contents of this book, you have expanded your awareness in ways that cannot be undone. There is no going back.

You now know that humanity is on the brink of disaster and it will be impossible for you to not pick-up the gauntlet and lead others in doing their part to save our planet.

Your Next Purpose

I allude to purpose quite often so it is helpful to define what this means and exactly why it is so relevant to helping us turn the tide for humanity.

There are a lot of misunderstandings about purpose, so I will first illuminate what it actually is and what it is not.

It is not tied to how you make your income. It can be, but it could also be completely unrelated.

It also does not have to be how you spend the majority of your time.

It is most definitely not what you felt called to do when you were in high school, unless that is now or within the past several years.

It does not end when you retire and may in fact just be fully matriculating into a clear path.

Your purpose will light you up and enable you to serve others in a meaningful way.

And it will evolve as you do. This means that at age twenty, you will have no idea how you will be called to serve others at forty, or when you are eighty.

Often we can be on our life's most aligned path and

working toward our purpose for quite some time. This is because we may need to acquire knowledge, resources or do certain things first.

We may experience a stream of perceived failures on different projects or possible new directions, where we learn something that we are meant to build on and continue progressing.

I mention this now because humanity is in a transitional time. It will require new leaders and new ways of doing things that could not have been envisioned several years ago.

Stay open to those divinely inspired ideas or nudges that come to you. No matter how fulfilling your purpose in life has been up until now, you will be called to expand it in new ways.

We are just getting started in this great, peaceful revolution.

Leadership is in Your DNA

I know you. You volunteered to be here at this particular juncture in human history. And a vast capacity for leadership was included in your programming. *It's in your DNA.*

Yes, that's part of the divine plan that each soul is given. In order to facilitate success in living your soul's path and purpose, your DNA includes specific programming that will contribute to your success.

Some people have a higher capacity for leadership, which is an ability to ethically influence others. Some people may have a predisposition for caregiving, healing, teaching, attention to detail, analysis and a host of other attributes; and most people have more than one of these.

You probably recognize some of your other skills or talents as you read that list. Most adults have an awareness of where their special interests and strengths lie.

But many are conditioned by their caregivers or culture to not acknowledge their innate ability to lead.

This may be due to a lack of self-love or self-esteem that was a result of childhood circumstances, or it could be attributed to cultural norms and expectations due to gender, socio-economic background or caste systems.

The programming from our circumstances is pervasive.

You may have been told or had it implied that you were not good enough. Perhaps you were compared to a sibling or other child in your neighborhood or extended family.

You may have adopted an identity of someone "not as bright" because you learned differently or had zero interest in the subject matter society compelled everyone to study.

You may have had it ingrained in you that you were "only

good for" or meant to raise children regardless of your interests or intellect. To be clear, raising children is a difficult and significant purpose, but it is not meant for everyone who is intended to lead elsewhere in society.

You may have been told that you have to work hard just to survive or that money does not grow on trees. Consequently, you developed a perspective of lack. You exhausted yourself with soul-sucking hours of mindless work, rather than pursuing your dreams or something with the potential of more fulfillment.

Your leadership ability has nothing to do with your background or current circumstances; but it will be influenced by your belief in yourself, and by your confidence and self-esteem.

If you hesitate to take action on anything suggested here, I recommend that you look more deeply at your capacity for self-love. Most of humanity can attribute their lack of action and silence to one of three things.

It is not due to a lack of caring but may be a lack of understanding, which we will discuss how to correct.

If it is not a lack of understanding, it may be an instinctual response to go into "freeze mode" which we have discussed. This simply requires awareness and a choice to move through it.

When one of these two issues is not at play, they are holding themselves back from taking action due to a lack of self-love, which leads to a lack of confidence. This is quite often the result of a bludgeoning their self-esteem took in childhood.

Globally, a vast majority of people believe that they love themselves. They are not aware or may be repressing the self-doubt and lack of esteem lingering in their subconscious.

This is an area that I know only too well. I speak from experience, knowing the prowess of our subconscious to repress painful memories. At the same time, it perpetuates distorted beliefs that were created by those repressed experiences.

As an adult, I believed for decades that I just had a poor memory. There was not much detail that I could recall from my childhood or teenage years. But as a victim of ongoing childhood emotional control and trauma, the perpetual cycle of being told I was not good enough had an effect well into adulthood. Even after becoming an experienced leader, I can look back and identify many decisions and relationships that were influenced by a need to prove my worth or be liked.

And this challenge is not unique to me. Billions around the globe from the full gamut of various cultures and socioeconomic backgrounds, suffer from a lack of self-love without recognizing the cause.

I developed competence at what I did and how I interacted with others, and so I appeared to be confident. True confidence does not come from competence, however, it comes from self-esteem.

A lack of self-love is insidious, and developing more of it

is a lifelong journey. Even if you have worked on this area of growth before, if you are hesitating now, that is a clue that there is more work to do. There is some level of anxiety, fear or lack of self-esteem and worth that is behind your hesitation. Even though fear of doing something different is instinctual, it is your identity, which includes your self-worth and esteem, that will allow you to trust yourself to do something new.

Ego-led vs. Egoless Leadership

Every human has an ego which is defined as our sense of self. This is not a bad thing in and of itself. It contributes to our ability to see ourselves as a unique individual who can function autonomously.

This has worked against us in numerous ways, however. Being separate and unique does not mean that we are not also a part of the whole. In our conversation about ecosystems, you will remember that we are all interconnected and our actions often have far reaching repercussions that we never actually see or identify.

Just because you do not see it, does not mean it is not there. We are all a part of the human ecosystem. We must make choices that remember and take that connectedness and importance of others into account.

We currently have a global leadership crisis because many of our globe's political leaders have an ego-led style. They have placed themselves and their personal advantage at the center of their goals and actions. Sometimes this is intentional, but often they do not even recognize it because their ego has led them throughout their life. It will impact what they say and do because they want to be well received or somehow grow their own significance. An example of this would be prioritizing a title or position over what you had to promise to get there. I am sure you can think of many examples of this if you have observed or participated in politics for a while.

When I say that we need egoless leaders, I am referring to what motivates them. Are they motivated by title, recognition and prestige? Are they motivated by approval ratings?

Or are they making decisions and guiding actions that are moving people and policies in a positive direction that is for the good of all?

You can not be concerned with progress for our communal greatest good and at the same time worry about being liked or popular. You can not advocate for massive change and at the same time worry about the response of constituents who will always resist change. The progress that we need to make in order to save the planet from climate change will not be popular with the masses. It will be inconvenient and expensive and that will not be popular with anyone.

But if the popular lack of action does not save us from extinction, being popular will not matter, will it?

The Rise of Feminine Leadership

Before you skip to the next section, allow me to clarify that this has nothing to do with women versus men. I am referring to the qualities that are historically thought of as masculine vs. feminine. Each of us has the ability to embrace all of those qualities; and we must, if we are to harmoniously and powerfully fulfill our potential as leaders. We are meant to balance the best of both the masculine and feminine attributes in order to reach our most optimal and productive leadership and life potential.

Think of the Chinese symbol from Taoism, the yin and yang emblem. It symbolizes both the light and dark. The male and female are part of one spectrum and compliment each other. They work in harmony to complete the circle.

Similarly, we are meant to blend the male and female characteristics to complete the whole leader.

Many of the leadership characteristics that are considered to be male are essential to any leader. This includes the adroitness of fast decision making and a perspective that looks for facts to analyze and synthesize. It includes a preference for precision and detail. These are all valuable traits to have instilled in our leaders.

But where would our world be without the attributes of leadership that are identified as more feminine? This includes qualities such as compassion and empathy, strong communication skills and an ability to facilitate consensus building. It includes imagination which leads to outside of the box thinking and innovation.

As it happens, we do not have to wonder where the world would be without a balance of these feminine attributes in leaders, because we are living the reality of it right now.

When our world leaders are willing to put ego aside and lead with love and compassion for humanity, we will see the end of the shortage of resources that leads to entire regions being sick or hungry.

Let us take a moment to think about some of the greatest leaders our world has known. It does not require recognition to be a great leader. There are many, past and present, who remain unknown; but for the purpose of illustration, I will mention a couple you may have heard about.

Socrates was a leader before his time. During a period when an authoritarian leadership style was the norm, he taught his students the value of questions, listening and deep thought. Listening and being open to other people's perspectives requires empathy and compassion and is a precursor for an evolving understanding. Socrates led by example and taught his students to love and respect others and be open to differing perspectives.

Martin Luther King Jr. is another great leader who comes to mind. He was able to blend male and female attributes into a potent combination of strengths that were unable to be ignored. It is clear from his communication style that he was decisive and able to speak with authority, but we also know from his stance of activism without violence that he led with heart. He was full of compassion for others, regardless of their race or socioeconomic backgrounds; and he encouraged others to follow his lead. He established environments where all felt like they were heard and that their voice mattered. And his ability to influence others stemmed not just from his oratory skills, but his understanding of people's differences and his compassion for what others may be experiencing.

This is the type of leadership that our world needs. When the globe's leaders are able to control their emotions and subjugate their own short term wins for long term gains, there will be more listening and consensus building, and the world will know peace.

When the world's leadership embraces significant innovations rather than corporate greed or fear of the blow back from unpopular decisions, the global community will come to experience the systemic changes necessary to save the planet.

The world does not need more female leaders per se, but we do need strong and spiritually guided men and women who are willing to do what is right over what is popular, convenient or self-serving.

I would equate this to the tough love necessary for a nurturing parenting style. When you love a child, you recognize that it is not always in their best interest to give them everything they want. It is not in the best interest of humanity to continue to allow the global community to deny climate change and resist the actions necessary to save us from ourselves. It is convenient and more lucrative for the short term, but *not* in our best interest.

The world needs more wise, tough and
compassionate leaders who are willing to do the
unpopular things that are in the
best interest of the collective.

Building Leadership Confidence

Many confuse confidence with the comfort level they
have built through competence. These are two different
things.

You are confident when you are able to move past any
natural hesitation or fear of doing something new, or
outside of your current comfort zone.

Confidence allows you to trust that even when things
don't work out as desired, you will be fine. You know that
you are resilient and able to recover from any
unexpected circumstances or undesired outcomes.

Beyond developing your self-love, the number one way to
instill this level of confidence in yourself is to develop and
learn to trust your inner wisdom. When you know you are
taking the most aligned actions for your life's path, you
will uplevel your identity and your ability to speak up for
what you believe in. You will unequivocally be the leader
you were created to be.

Most people in first world cultures have been raised to
doubt their guidance. Your inner wisdom is with you your

entire life and meant to guide you on your soul's path and purpose. Many refer to this as intuition and recognize it as their inspired ideas that seem to come out of nowhere. When you learn to strengthen that communication, it will instill a new level of confidence in your action taking.

If you know you are on your life's intended path and taking the most aligned actions to live a fulfilled life in service to humanity, why would you question your direction or hesitate in your action? Why would you be afraid of failure or judgment of others? You would not.

When you develop a strong trust in your guidance and commitment to your path, those insecurities will fall away. And when your actions do not produce the results you desire immediately, which is often the case, you will view the experience as it is, without projections or judgment.

You will glean the necessary feedback from it, adjust your course, and be undeterred in the pursuit of your big vision and the direction that you have been guided to pursue.

The confidence that comes from honing your connection with your inner guidance and becoming crystal clear on your path and next actions, is life and trajectory changing.

The world and future of humanity requires each one of us to step out of our existing circumstances and comfort zones, and into the leadership roles we were born to fulfill.

Your way does not have to match my way,
as long as we lead with love.

Differentiators in Transformative Communication

Each of us has examples of challenging people in our lives that can be distilled into leadership lessons.

Whether it was an overly ego-centric boss or a committee chair who wouldn't listen or take ownership of directing a meeting, there are many bad examples that come to mind.

I remember having a boss once who was so self-absorbed that his staff considered him to be an egomaniac. His ego seemed to linger after he left a room; and his style of doing business, which I refrain from referring to as leadership, taught me more than all of the better examples I had observed could have. It was early in my management journey and he gave me a clear insight into poor practices to avoid.

He looked down on women and minimized the

contributions we made. I recognized this because I am female, but would hazard a guess that many other types of people who were different from him would be treated similarly. He was an example of someone looking to have his existing beliefs reinforced. He chose not to listen to differing viewpoints, demonstrating a belief that other perspectives from his own were lacking in value.

He utilized an authoritative style of communication and entered every conversation with the intention of making himself look good as he dictated directives to others. In other words, he did not listen and was not open to other people's ideas or the possibility that someone else could contribute to a solution. Not only did his style contribute to discouragement, disempowerment and a high turnover in the workforce, but it led to stagnation and mediocrity in the goods and services being delivered.

We see what does not work all around us; and if you look closely, you can also observe what works. A teacher who keeps a tight but nurturing reign in their classroom or a waiter who confidently guides you through an ordering dilemma are good examples.

And in your own family dynamics you may find daily examples, if you observe the relationship dance among all of your family members. You may observe an elderly family member who rules with a tight fist and demands that their way wins, or a child who manages to eloquently negotiate for their cause and be rewarded in some manner.

We all have an ability to lead or influence in any relationship that we are a part of; and your influence will be amplified if you understand the other person and adapt your approach to your conversations accordingly.

Dominance vs. Influence

Leadership is a deep topic and many of the nuances are beyond the scope of this book. One area that will help you gain significant traction, however, is your ability to *connect* with the other person and communicate your point persuasively.

Many people think of a leader as someone who is always in control and dominating the discussions and plan development; but that is the antithesis of a leader. That would be a dictator.

**There is no room for dominance
or ego in leadership.**

A predisposition to be in charge or to always be in control is a sign of a weak leader with a sizable lack of self-esteem. If you look at the world political stage, I am sure a few examples will come to your mind.

Effective leaders put ego aside and prioritize open communication and collaboration.

And they are great listeners. This is because leadership at its core is our ability to ethically guide another person or group and you cannot do that if you do not understand them. We must be curious and ask questions with the sincere desire to understand other viewpoints and perspectives, rather than just sway someone to ours.

We lead when we are able to shape the development of a new viewpoint or incite someone into taking action; and you do not have to have a title or be directing the conversation to do that. If you are contributing to building a consensus that is in everyone's best interest, you are leading.

You may have heard expressions that refer to leading from behind or from the side. When you put ego aside, you realize that there is often more value to be with or behind the team observing and allowing others to have autonomy in making their own way

Think of it like a shepherd herding their flock. If you are in front showing them the way, how will you know if one of them wanders off and gets lost? You will not know. That is why shepherds do not position themselves in front of the flock.

To be clear, someone has to take a position in front in many situations, and if you are comfortable in doing so that may be your path. But if the situation calls for that kind of leadership, do not forget to listen for signals behind you and check the rear-view mirror. The captain of a large ship may be at the helm; but they also maintain open communication with other areas of the ship, such as the engine room, where information from elsewhere may impact their progress. In this scenario, the captain may be considered to be in front; but they will cultivate the necessary systems to be aware of information coming in from other directions as well.

The idea of leadership can scare or put off many people, but it does not need to. The takeaway here is that you do not need to catapult yourself onto the platform or in front of the crowd to be able to contribute and lead in a valuable way.

Do not take your ability to influence others lightly.

Every conversation is an opportunity to share information and influence that other person's awareness. And if you feel like you are not effective in influencing others, then I invite you to look at this as a growth opportunity.

The ability to communicate persuasively is a skill that everyone can master if they are willing to do the work.

I remember being in a room of managers one time, who had been brought together to solve an operational problem. The challenge was that many in the room just wanted to hear themselves talk and flex their knowledge and position. No one seemed to be listening to each other and consequently, nothing was accomplished. I was a junior manager at the time, and stayed quiet while marveling at the ineffective use of time by adults who were supposed to have a common goal.

This type of behavior is common. People want to prove what they know and be "right," and quite often lose sight of the overriding purpose of the conversation or the challenge that they are supposed to be solving.

As I recall, there were more than a few who restated their existing knowledge and position on the topic more than once, and asked zero questions of anyone else. They wanted to exert their authority and dominate the conversation, and seemed to be OK with walking out of that meeting no further along toward solving the problem than when it started.

Adapting Your Communication Style

If there is one undeniable truth that helps everyone communicate and lead more adeptly, it is an understanding that people prefer to communicate in different ways; and your ability to recognize their preferences rather than pushing your preferred style and way of communicating onto them, will eliminate barriers to your message being heard.

As an example, some people speak with a very fast clip and dislike waiting for someone with a slower pace to get information out. This results in frustration and their listening and ability to process what is being said shuts down.

Everyone is most comfortable relating and speaking with people who are similar to themselves.

This goes well beyond superficial appearances, beliefs, education or socioeconomic status. If you present your information in their preferred format, they are more likely to be open to it.

Leadership is the opposite of pushing ideas on others and forcing them to acquiesce. Before you can influence someone, they need to be open to receiving your communication.

This is a deep topic, but here are some top tips to get you started:

1. When you are communicating with another person, recognize their pace of speech and general processing speed. Then speed up or slow down your presentation in a natural way, to come closer to meeting them where they are. Note that you want to feel natural in doing this and just by recognizing their preferences and what is natural to them, you will naturally begin to adapt your pace.

2. Ask for their preferred way to communicate. Some people just want a reader's digest version, meaning they prefer that you give them a quick recap. Others who like to take their time and analyze information are likely to prefer that you send them written articles or data that they can peruse, digest and perhaps do their own research before coming to their own conclusions.

3. Ask if they would like more details or just an overview, if you are not sure. Most people will appreciate your deference to their learning and analysis style.

In all transparency, this is a skill that requires ongoing development. It is worth everyone's time and effort however, because we must break down the barriers that are usually erected when asked to consider new information or different perspectives. Developing this skill will enable you to build rapport more quickly. Some people will be very easy to approach and build rapport with because they are similar to you. Others, no matter how long you have worked on this skill, will continue to challenge you.

A necessary attribute is to be persistent. Continue sharing your message, even when you hit roadblocks along the way. People do not like to hear anything that is in opposition to their current beliefs and paradigms.

Remember that any resistance you come up against has nothing to do with you. It is their natural survival instincts activating to keep them safe, by blocking new ideas and information.

Quite often these people just need more time. No one intentionally holds onto false beliefs and narratives. When you share information in a non threatening way, you are opening the door to broaden their awareness. Do not be disappointed if they are not receptive immediately; but also, do not give up on them.

Conveying this information is not for the purpose of simply broadening your knowledge. I am proposing that everyone reading this chooses to actively develop communication skills that enable the effective sharing of information with people of differing viewpoints. Specifically, so that each of you can share the hard reality of our current circumstances with everyone you meet.

Sharing will be relatively easy, but sharing does no good if people remain closed to hearing or believing the information you share.

Your presentation and method of delivery matters.

We must continue to chip away at the misinformation and resistance by approaching the sharing of information in non threatening and compatible ways. It is too important to be dissuaded by a few naysayers and pockets of climate change denial. If a majority of the world's populace continues to ignore the real data and destruction we are now seeing, we will soon be out of time to turn this tide.

We must each do the work to build rapport and take advantage of every opportunity to share the facts of our tenuous circumstances.

Invite local community members to brainstorm with you on what immediate needs you can impact.

Join an advocacy group and look for ways that your unique skill set can contribute to a larger cause. And if you do not have time, find some money to donate; or better yet, do both.

The world cannot wait for us to figure out how to reverse the tide on the accelerating impact of global warming, without any disruption or inconvenience.

We have to meet our planet where it is now, and take massive action rather than baby steps.

Ignoring climate change is no longer an option, and the immediate goal and impetus is not creating the beautiful future that I have enumerated here. The immediate goal must be to ensure that we have a future at all.

Truth & Consequences

Truth must be sought, and it is almost always different from our perception.

Perceptions are how we view the world as we filter it through our past experiences, programs and paradigms. They rarely align exactly with truth, and yet we cling to them and argue for them as if they do.

We must each actively seek the truth.

Know that what you hear from the world's media outlets is filtered through the writer or speaker's perceptions.

Know that what is shared is frequently only a piece of the full story. There are almost always additional ways that one situation can be interpreted, and those alternate perspectives do not typically get shared.

Much of the media is littered by distortions of the truth, so you cannot rely solely on similar sources for your information. Seek out knowledge from subject matter experts who don't have something to gain financially from the information they share.

Seek information from a variety of sources with differing viewpoints so the "truth" can be pieced together from all of the variations heard.

And then check in with your inner wisdom.

When you release attachment to any pre-existing beliefs you have held and sit quietly with the different perspectives, you will find the truth. It may take time to sift through all of the distortions, but the truth will resonate.

It may not match your previous beliefs, but you will know it without being told.

Think about a time when you knew something without having been told. There was no obvious or scientific reason that you knew it, but you just knew it.

We have all experienced something like this before. For me, the most obvious example I can remember, prior to developing my clair senses, was when I was pregnant with our fourth child. There were complications with the baby and a number of possible diagnoses with scary outcomes were discussed with us. The potential scenarios did not send me into a spiral of fear, however. I already "knew" what was wrong with her, and it was not the dreaded worst case scenario. There was no possible way that I could know this, but I did.

You might call it mother's intuition but it was actually claircognizance. I knew that the scarier circumstance did not apply and that I would have a child born with Down Syndrome. Because of this comforting reassurance, I was able to avoid being plagued by additional terminal scenarios and "what ifs" that were proffered to us.

Every person has the ability to develop their inner knowing or claircognizance.

It is a skill that everyone is able to hone and it is the only way to accurately discern the facts from fiction when you are surrounded by sensationalistic journalism and a hype driven culture. Many media outlets are focused on what sells rather than researching and conveying facts in an objective manner.

If you doubt that this is the case with your favorite news outlet, here is a simple test. Look at five headlines they generated recently. Creating appealing headlines is a science and most organizations have professionals who spin a topic in a way that will get their audience to click on their article or watch their video. This usually involves appealing to what their target audience wants to hear, by validating their existing beliefs rather than sharing facts.

Are the headlines of your favorite media source impartial or appearing to appeal to a specific audience?

Most people will screen what they give their attention to, based on whether it is a match for their current paradigms. If the news headline does not hint at reinforcing their current beliefs, many will not read or watch the news story.

In regards to global warming, the consequence of being misled by a plethora of inaccurate or intentionally spun information is analogous to sheep being led to slaughter.

We are currently seeing and living through the consequences of the majority of our population not discerning and acting on climate change facts and truth. It is convenient and therefore a normal human reaction to want to believe that climate change is not real, or that the impact is overly hyped.

Do not take the proffered news or friend's social media shares for granted. Do your research and question everything.

Action creates inspiration which leads to more action. You just have to start.

Hope for our Future

Sometimes we see things transpire around us that we knew were inevitable, and at other times circumstances are a surprise and seem to morph into existence from out of nowhere. In some circumstances, we resign ourselves to change because a situation evolves in a way that appears to be out of our control.

The devolution of our environment and ongoing destruction of life on the planet is none of these situations.

It is not currently expected because the bulk of humanity continues to keep blinders on and deny the reality of our circumstances.

It is also not a surprise because scientists have been alerting us with copious warnings about the disastrous outcomes of climate change for decades.

And yet here we are.

Learning to adapt and synthesize new technology in responsible ways is a part of the evolutionary process that we have not figured out yet.

We have also discussed the predictable pattern of people avoiding anything that requires change or inconvenience.

But we have not yet elaborated the simple process you can use to help turn the tide. Small changes have been implemented in various regions and more positive adaptations are continuously innovated; but many believe that the massive shifts and changes necessary to reverse our trajectory seem like an overwhelming and unattainable goal.

When Thomas Edison embraced a vision to create a bulb of light, it seemed like an overwhelming and crazy idea without a clear path forward. Rather than sitting at his desk scribbling formulas and trying to figure out the best way to make it work, he was compelled to just start. As those who have heard the story are aware, it was not a quick process and it required persistence to keep going after one experiment after another proved futile.

But he held his vision and kept trying. He would never have been able to distill the process into something that actually worked without having started.

Before the final steps of a complex process can be fully envisioned, the process has to actually start. There will be many learning opportunities from the so-called failed attempts as we struggle to get traction. With each attempt there will be more knowledge and experience gained, helping to bolster the next attempt.

When starting, Edison was not able to fully enumerate how he would create that working and replicable bulb; but he understood that scribbling plans and discussing ideas will only illuminate so much of the process.

To visualize the entire path we must first start, then learn and adjust tactics while in action.

Every large new obstacle is like that until it has been navigated successfully, and this challenge is no different. We cannot possibly know all of the steps to correct our environmental crises; but we have to start taking more meaningful, trajectory shifting action before the next steps will become evident. Only after we start taking bold action will we become aware of all of the unforeseen obstacles. The most judicious next steps will come to light as we move through the process.

There is no going back, only forward, which means working with our current circumstances and what we know the causes to be.

In order to stem the tide of pain from climate change, it is an obligation of the few who are aware, to spread this critical awareness to those still in denial.

An overwhelming task becomes manageable when there are many hands working together with limited resistance.

I am not suggesting that we will need to get to a point of no resistance; but we know that resistance slows progress and the less there is, the more accelerated the change will be.

So how do we spread awareness and limit the resistance to change?

We Rise and Fall Together

There is no way to soften this, so I'll be blunt. Being liked as a leader is overrated.

We have fallen on the sword to placate the desires of the masses, rather than leading with the tough love that humanity needed.

Many countries have implemented the ideal of democracy in a destructive manner. It is important to understand the desires of society, but the needs of a populace are often different and cannot be delivered when leaders are overly focused on the short term "wants" of their constituents or the special interest groups who got them elected.

As explored earlier, it is a bit like the difference between overly indulgent versus firm and loving parenting. Those who grow up being overly indulged by well meaning caregivers who do not have time or the capacity to enforce what is in their greatest good, do not fare as well as those raised by caregivers who do. Leaders who take the easier path of supplying what is wanted rather than needed and for the greatest good of that community, are achieving short term wins often at the expense of giving up on the longer term gain.

We saw an example of this style of visionary leadership when President Roosevelt led the United States out of the Great Depression. There was a culmination of circumstances that led to the eventual market crash and financial upheaval that reverberated around the globe. The multiple levels of impact and human suffering from this one event were profound and when President Roosevelt took office, recovery seemed elusive.

Roosevelt was unconcerned about the popular desires of his constituents and had many who criticized his programs. Undeterred, he implemented innovative ideas to create new jobs and stimulate the economy with new growth. His plans held strategies that were unpopular with many; but the result was a faster turnaround of the economy than had been believed possible.

It is analogous to the metaphor of giving someone a fish versus teaching them how to fish. Leaders must always keep an eye on the long term vision and greatest good of all, rather than the short term and easiest "bandaid" that often does not stop the bleeding.

Visionary leaders do not choose the easiest path. They blaze trails that create solutions in the highest good for all.

There are both good news and challenges inherent in being part of a bigger community or society.

It means that there are brilliant minds generating new

and creative ideas continuously, to aid this challenge; and there are resources available to activate the most probable solutions. That is good news because if everyone was on their own to figure it out, the probability of each individual arriving at a viable solution and being able to put it into action would be nil.

As a global community, we have the added benefit of the mastermind. Napoleon Hill famously said that when two or more minds come together for the purpose of generating a solution, the sum of that combination is far greater than each mind individually. One mind plays off the other to come up with something better than any single mind could do alone.

This is the power of working together in collaboration and community. We can come up with better solutions, and build more traction in the implementation of those solutions; and we can wear down the resistance faster.

There is another expression that "there is one in every group" which implies that there will always be a dissenter or so-called trouble maker. This is the benefit and challenge of free choice. Everyone can choose what to believe.

*The larger problem is when people **choose not to think** for themselves.*

This arises when people allow unethical and greedy pundits and distortions from hype focused media outlets to tell them what to think.

*It is God's will that every human have free choice but **not*** *that they abdicate responsibility for thinking.*

The planet is in this current predicament because the majority of the population have abdicated responsibility for their thinking.

They have chosen to believe the easiest narratives that require the least change and inconvenience. This means that they have chosen to believe the toxic industry generated lies about global warming. They want to believe that it is a made-up ploy which should be ignored because this is the easiest message to believe. It allows them to continue in their current routines without interruption. There is no need to change habits or buying patterns if climate change is a hoax.

The solution involves enlightening more of this vast segment of the population about the problem. They cannot be reached through the media because everyone will continue to listen to or read news from sources that reinforce their current beliefs.

The only way to reach more people is to have more of us who are informed, talking openly about it.

As we have seen on the world stage through various national politics, just because information is shared does not mean everyone is paying attention and listening to that information. The answer has to start with low conflict information sharing of facts that are hard to ignore.

Every thinking person can come to their own conclusions when facts are shared in a non threatening manner.

Some will choose not to listen but many will rethink their stance, because the reality of harsh circumstances being created by climate change will continue and become harder to ignore.

The benefits of being part of the global community are tremendous. No one is alone in the fight and the best and brightest minds on the planet are working to create new and sustainable solutions.

The drawback in being part of a global community is that it requires a majority of the populace supporting substantive changes, in order for the necessary turnaround to be realized.

As our conversation about ecosystems highlights, we are each interconnected. Each one of us plays an integral role in the success of this movement.

Responsibility of Choice

We are at a crossroads; and our world will only have relief when we end the widespread unethical business practices, corporate greed and the current broken political systems. We have to either accept the challenge and change, or continue to allow greed to rule our world and kill it in short order.

Most people would choose the former, but do not know how to help. How can one person contribute and help turn around this march to global extinction?

Every individual has the freedom of choice.

This can work in our favor; but most of the time it hampers our progress instead, because the vast majority of people choose comfort over what is right - ninety-eight percent of the time.

The first order of business for you and everyone you know, is to help enlighten the rest of the population to our plight. First things must be first and saving humanity needs to be the priority for every person on the planet right now.

If you are not in immediate peril due to floods, drought or other climatic trauma, it is easy to ignore the state of the world and continue with business as usual.

Do not do that. Each individual on this planet is essential to its protection and continued existence; and *ignoring the destructive course we are on is tantamount to being complicit in causing its extinction.*

When the silent majority speak up and demand action from our governments to reverse this devastation, our trajectory will correct course quickly.

That is the *good news and hope* we can each hold on to.

**When the uninvolved majority become engaged,
our future will be saved.**

It is that simple. But it will not be easy to orchestrate because people hate to be inconvenienced almost as much as they hate and resist change.

Many Ways to Help

If you are still wavering on how to help, I have outlined some simple ways here. This is not a comprehensive list but will serve as a place to start. As a responsible steward and conscious leader, there are actually many ways that one person can make a significant difference.

The first would be to educate yourself and everyone you know on our increasingly disastrous circumstances.

Do your research and become active and vocal in advocating for necessary changes in your local area. We need changes on a global scale, but that can feel intimidating and block you from taking action. Start locally and as you find areas that you are passionate about assisting with, you can broaden your efforts from there if you feel called to do so. If each community did their part, we would experience the global shift necessary to save our planet.

Bring it up in every conversation. Our planet and all of humanity are headed for extinction. Given the gravity of our circumstances, this should be a topic for discussion in every interaction.

Educate and recruit all of your friends, family and acquaintances to join you or to find their own ways to create an impact. Saving the planet should be at the top of everyone's mind and yet it's not a common topic of conversation in most circles. You can help change that by making it a primary topic of yours.

TIP:

People do not like to be told what to think. Be diplomatic and open the door to questions and exploring possibilities if this is not a topic they welcome. Saving the planet is more important than being liked so you do not have to sugar coat anything. Leading with facts and then asking questions will allow others to come to their own conclusions and is a powerful strategy. This is as opposed to the more common tendency of dictating thoughts and expecting others to embrace them.*

Inventory your interests and skills. You do not need to be an environmental scientist to contribute necessary skills to this fight. Ask yourself what area of the environmental crisis you are most passionate about helping with and what skills you enjoy utilizing.

As an example, you may have more of an affinity for water and ocean life, air quality, eliminating deforestation, or reducing carbon emissions. And when you think about how you can help with one of these areas, you may determine that you are really good at communicating and educating. Or perhaps recruiting and organizing volunteer efforts is your forte. Or you may feel compelled to craft and advocate for legislation that will impact necessary improvements.

Join a local advocacy group and become politically active if you are not already. It does not matter what country you live in, every government should have the planet front and center on its agenda. And if they do not, vote in a new one.

The world's governments are leading us to ruin due to the lack of a mandate from their constituents, their lack of egoless leadership and a lack of focus on this biggest priority. There are some well meaning politicians of course, and some positive initiatives have been undertaken in a couple of progressive nations; but there are not enough of them to elicit meaningful change. Too many government leaders are crippled by their fear of losing votes and corporate money for their next campaign.

We can turn the tide. And we have to.

The systems in place do not just need tweaks. They need to be completely rebuilt. Systems are only good for as long as they serve us; and when they no longer serve, they need to change. Political systems and environmental regulation around the world are long overdue for an overhaul, because time is running out.

Identify the biggest needs in your community and go to work. You could run for office, with the environment at the center of your platform.

If the planet dies, none of those other issues will matter.

If the billions of politically uninvolved people in our world were to become aware and raise their voices in concern, things would change.

Start anywhere, with anything that interests you. Do not overthink or over complicate it. It can be overwhelming to look at the big picture and all that is required. Just start with one area and one action that you can take right away that will help make a small contribution to a worthy cause.

As you start taking action, more ideas or inspiration may come to you that you can act on; but do not try to see your entire path before you begin.

Just start. Start as small as you need to get past any resistance and overthinking. These are both common reactions to watch for, so that you are able to adroitly move past them.

Just start NOW.

The world cannot wait for us to get more organized or find convenient ways to welcome change. The changes may be messy or painful, but necessary to our survival. And survival of our species, along with all of the other species on the planet, seems like a compelling reason to take the hard actions now.

To turn the tide, we must start by informing a lot more people of the truth, and incite action on a massive scale globally.

*Sample conversation starters about climate change and the necessity to take action:

"Have you noticed how the weather has been consistently warmer? Did you know that the global temperature has reached all time highs each of the past two years?"

If their response is doubtful, you might offer to share some statistics or research. If they are engaged, you could follow-up with additional information you have accumulated, such as:

"If this trajectory isn't reversed, it will be too hot for most of life on the planet to survive in a very short time."

Do not be in a rush. Allow them to do their own research or to think about what you shared if necessary. There will be very few ready to join you in your efforts on your first conversation. Give them time, and set a reminder in your calendar to follow-up with another conversation and/or an invitation to get involved.

For conversations with people already aware of the crisis, you might consider going deeper:

"What are your favorite ways to limit carbon emissions?"

"Did you know that the primary contributor to the rising emissions and Greenhouse Effect is the utility industries, followed closely by the transportation industries? If we switch to solar power and eliminate all unnecessary travel and shipping, the emission contributions would be reduced by over 80% annually and completely turn around the rising temperatures and our escalating crisis."

You do not have to memorize or stress over the details. Share from your heart and if they have questions you cannot answer, you can invite them to do some research to share with you because you are still learning.

Movements are created when the
silent majority are activated.

The Domino Effect

After four decades of debate, we are now seeing a cascading domino effect with the earth's climate change symptoms. After decades of self-serving industrial evolution and destructive individual behaviors that have become habits, the effects are gaining scope and velocity.

Years ago, no one had and therefore did not miss the convenience of a microwave oven. When microwaves were first introduced there was a learning and adaptation curve, as people were not sure if this new appliance would even prove useful. Now we know that when exposure is sustained over time, the electromagnetic waves emanating from a microwave are bad for human health. And yet the majority of households in first world countries still choose to utilize microwaves because they have become accustomed to them. People tend to avoid inconvenience and stay with what they know.

In a myriad of circumstances, many choose to ignore the potential for ill effects from products and behaviors that have proven long term risks, rather than giving up the short term convenience they have grown accustomed to and enjoy.

This behavior can also often be attributed to what is known as the herd mentality. One of our survival instincts compels us to look for and emulate the behavior of others. The inferred conclusion being that if others are doing it, they must know what they are doing and it is safe and desirable.

The first world is overflowing with examples of known carcinogens that are still in use by a majority of the population. It is easier to skip researching topics and continue with societal norms. It is easier to turn a blind eye to potential future consequences, rather than change existing habits.

It is easier, but potentially deadly.

You are probably wondering what the planet's devolution from climate change has to do with a microwave. It is the same, predictable human behavior wherever it is applied.

People resist change unless they see
an immediate benefit in it.

In general, most people are not good at engaging in short term deprivation, effort or inconvenience for a long term desired gain. The predominance of obesity in modern society is another example of this.

In the case of our catastrophic world order, it is going to require a global commitment to embracing both short and long term strategies. These strategies will perpetuate inconvenience for many, because of the behavioral changes they will require by both industries and individuals. It will require discipline and focus on the long term goal rather than short term comfort.

The choice appears to be easy, until we consider the denial of climate change by supposed leaders and authorities. When trusted authorities insist that the actions to limit global warming are unnecessary, the majority of their constituents believe them because it is way easier than the alternative.

Misinformation proliferated by the greedy and self-serving, assures the public that the changing and extreme weather patterns are an anomaly, or a man made creation for the advancement of opposing political agendas.

When there is conflicting information available, people will always choose to believe that which is easiest or supports their current beliefs and narratives.

In summary, we know that humans are programmed to avoid or resist change, and they will gravitate to information and solutions that allow for the least amount of interference in their current lives. If you tell someone there is no such thing as climate change, that supports their desire to not change anything in their current circumstances and behaviors. Therefore, it is predictable that the majority of people on the planet would desire to believe that climate change is a hoax so that they can hold on to their existing habits and circumstances.

Regulation and Shifting Perceptions

Because people will believe what they most want to hear, an early step in this process must be to limit the spread of misinformation. Unethical media outlets and the proliferation on the internet of mistruths shared as facts and news, have led to an uneducated and misled general public.

All solutions must start with the world's governments, of course. The media outlets are run as businesses rather than a not for profit source of journalism as they should be. If we are to correct the current proliferation of lies, slandering and "fake news," the profit motive of the businesses needs to be eliminated. There is a strong propensity to share what their target audience wants to hear, because that benefits their audience reach which in turn impacts their bottom line.

In some of the world's media sources you will find news that is full of conjecture and hyperbole, leading their audiences off the cliff of radical journalistic abuse.

It was not always like this, of course. Prior to the current proliferation of opinion outlets, the entire industry of journalism held itself to a high standard of caution and fact checking in order to report unbiased news.

That has changed as the wealth generation by those businesses began to take precedence over accurate and fair journalism. Then the downward spiral of news media as entertainment and an audience magnet began.

Much of the world values freedom of speech, but at what point should it be monitored and misinformation regulated? There are many instances when public safety is at risk, and the media and social platforms involved must be responsible and held accountable for the misinformation they enable.

There is truth in the argument that most adults should be able to discern fact from fiction and do their own filtering of information; but when fiction is presented as fact, it is unreasonable to expect the majority of the population to understand what the facts actually are.

There is a need to develop more aggressive regulation to protect individuals from manipulation by the wealthy minority who control most of the world's media outlets and are propelled by greed.

The distortions and mistruths are created intentionally by those who want to manipulate the public and prevent change.

This type of manipulation must become illegal if we are to turn the tide toward truth and a healthy planet. If a statement cannot be supported, it should be clearly labeled as an opinion rather than fact. This simple but necessary requirement would not limit anyone's free speech, but it would protect the trusting majority from unwittingly believing and proliferating other people's opinions as fact.

New regulations will not fix everything that is not working, however.

We need to create a global shift in perception.

The majority of those aware of global warming are under the false impression that the consequences of climate change can be solved by their governments. This has led to the multitude being hands off and waiting for the problem to be fixed by someone else.

It is this hands off approach by the majority of the planet's population that is enabling the disintegration of the planet's ecosystems.

Climate change is not our governments' problem. It is the problem of all global citizens.

Each and every person on the planet is impacted by the threat of climate change and *each of us is responsible for contributing to the solution.*

Those who already do, can do more; but it is the many who are silent and unengaged who are steering us toward destruction.

It is the majority who never question and blindly trust their government leaders to figure things out and do the right thing, who are now the most culpable. Some government leaders are trying, but they are up against insurmountable odds because there are not enough of them willing to do what is right. And so we hear the clamor of climate change denial grow.

And all of humanity loses.

Globally, we must do a better job with outreach. We must educate the masses and encourage them to weigh in on this life threatening issue.

This may sound impossible to implement. How can the currently uninvolved, be compelled to become involved?

It starts with communication and education.

> *People do not turn a deaf ear to*
> *important issues intentionally.*

They are under false assumptions that it is not an issue, that someone else can take care of it, or that their one lone voice will not make a difference.

They do not understand the potential of percentages and the ripple effect.

The Law of Percentages

If one person educates themselves on the climate crisis and then shares some research and the importance of what they learned with others, it is reasonable to assume that at a minimum half of those people will be concerned or at least intrigued to learn more.

The law of averages will work in our favor if each person reading this book shares from their heart to helpfully inform and engage just four people. At least two of those people will be intrigued to learn more or compelled to act on the information.

And when those two people reach out to at least four friends each, that will equate to at least four more people informed and acting on this information by sharing it with others.

 And when they each share with four people, that is at least another eight people who will be inspired to be involved. If you are doing the math, that ripple has spread to fifteen people from you, our reader, sharing some compelling information with just four people.

That is the beauty of percentages and the ripple effect. And of course, you and many others may know way more than just four people that you would like to inspire… which compounds the ripple.

This is why your voice, and that of everyone you know, matters more than you think.

It is not just how we vote that will make the required changes possible. It is how we communicate about these important issues and other life affirming decisions that will be made, as we co-create a new era with our communities.

Your Actions Ignite Your Belief

We become who we believe ourselves to be.

This may come across as a "chicken versus the egg" conundrum; but stick with me, because your actions will always come first.

Beliefs are the antithesis to acquired knowledge and skills. It does not matter what or how much you learn; until you believe that you are the person capable of doing something or creating that thing, you will never be that person. You may try, but will be sorely disappointed in your lack of progress and stymied results.

Integrity in your identity informs your results.

If your identity is out of alignment with your goal, you will never be able to create it; and your identity evolves from your beliefs, rather than from your acquired knowledge and skills.

You may not recognize all of your beliefs because many of them were formed in childhood before you reached the age of reasoning. Before you had any filters to interpret what you saw or heard, your beliefs sprung into existence based on your small child interpretations.

As an example, if a young child hears their parents fighting all of the time, they might form the belief that being in a marriage or partnership is a miserable experience; and subsequently as an adult they avoid experiencing a long term relationship with a partner.

Or a child could experience chastising and misdirected prodding from a well meaning adult who is trying to get them to apply themselves to an undertaking. Those experiences could easily transform into an adult belief and subsequent identity of being "never good enough."

You get the idea. Beliefs are insidious. You frequently will not know what they are, but they create who you are.

There was a gentleman named Artemis a few thousand years ago, whose story illustrates this concept well. Artemis lived in a hierarchical society, and was a peasant at the bottom of the hierarchy. His family had no means to speak of and often struggled to feed themselves. Because of his childhood circumstances, he formed a paradigm of lack and a perceived need to scramble for survival and horde scraps.

This instinctual response to his childhood environment served him well until his environment changed. You see, Artemis grew to become an extremely handsome man. He embodied the type of enviable physical attributes that they write about in odes and fairy tales. And this led to his own fairy tale unfolding in his life. He gained the attention of a princess in the local royal family and was invited to participate as a member of her court. This was a great honor for a young man of no means and he welcomed the opportunity.

But sadly, Artemis did not get to participate as part of her court for long. Although his circumstances had changed, his beliefs and identity had not. He still viewed the world through his lens of lack, and was soon caught stealing from the royal kitchen. That imploded to not only end his time at the court, but the young man's life.

His beliefs and identity were subconscious and did not uplevel as quickly as his new circumstances necessitated. Although he was gifted with abundance, he still identified as a starving peasant who needed to hustle to survive.

Your current identity is the result of your current beliefs; and in order to start that ripple, you may think you need to become someone you do not believe yourself to be.

But who you are is enough.

You do not have to be someone you are not. But you do need to be the you that you were created to be before the formation of your limiting beliefs.

The only way to do this is by taking action. Very small actions in the beginning is the best way to start, as this will limit the subconscious resistance you are likely to experience. When you act as the person who does not have all of those limiting beliefs and self-doubt holding them back, you begin to embrace the identity of that person. This is a real life scenario where "fake it until you make it" will reap rewards. When you pretend and take action as if you are someone who is confident in the pursuit of new goals, you will become that person.

A young man named Joseph applied this technique many years ago. He was raised in a middle class family and became a carpenter by trade. Although he was relatively happy with his profession of choice, he got a strong nudge or calling one day to be and do something different and more impactful. He sensed that he was meant to be a teacher for his next chapter; but he questioned the nudge and himself at that time because he was "just him". He didn't believe he was anything special and was just an "average Joe" who was too old to acquire so much new knowledge and move into a dramatically new direction.

As the nudge to pursue a career shift became stronger, it became hard to ignore and at the same time, scary to contemplate. Perhaps you can relate. His identity, as he knew it, was tied up in his profession and how he moved through the world on a daily basis. Pursuing a new career was, for him, a complete pivot in his life. Being paralyzed with fear and self-doubt, the only thing he knew to do was to start asking questions and researching possibilities. It was before the internet so this was a time consuming undertaking; but he committed to figuring out what the new knowledge, skills and potential paths would be for a pivot.

It may not surprise you to hear that once he began to research the situation, some of his fear dissipated. Before long, it didn't seem like such a novel and insurmountable task and he was able to clearly see what the next step would be. And then the next. It took him several years to acquire the necessary knowledge and acquaintances for a smooth career transition. But as he took those first couple of steps the belief in himself grew, and he began to see himself as that man who could step into and be successful in his new career path.

Although everyone is at a different point in their personal growth journey, being who you were born to be will probably entail taking an inventory of who you are not. Remember that you are not any of your roles or past experiences.

There is only one you and no one else can do what you are meant to do, in the way that you are meant to do it.

Your path is unique to you, and when you tap into your guidance and gain clarity and alignment with your soul's path and purpose, you'll create ripples of impact beyond what you currently believe you are capable of creating.

Very few have awakened to their actual purpose for this transitional phase of humanity. For most people reading this, you will soon find your purpose pivoting or expanding exponentially, as you follow your inner wisdom.

It will lead you to be the you that you were created to be, so that you can create the ripple that only you can create.

Not every purpose is meant to have magnitude in its scope. You could be meant to go deep in touching the lives of one or two people rather than thousands. And if you can do something to help that person in a significant way, that's enough and it will fulfill you. You will know you are living your most impactful life possible.

Once you become clear on your path, your identity will transform and uplevel in unimaginable ways because of the aligned actions you take.

That's the secret.

If your beliefs or identity are holding you back, you do not need to know exactly what they are and where the sticking point is. You just need to start taking action as the person you are meant to be. Take action as someone who holds the necessary beliefs and identity to create your goal.

When your subconscious sees you taking those actions, a shift happens.

And you become that person you were meant to be.

Aggressive action in times of crisis
has turned the tide throughout history.

Turning the Tide

From Looming Extinction to Evolution

You will probably experience doubt in yourself and your ability to contribute in the manner you feel guided to take action. This is because each of us is capable of far more than we have been raised and indoctrinated to believe. Each of us is here at this particular time in humanity's evolution for a purpose. To help with the process and serve others in some meaningful manner.

Because we have never seen a time like this, there is no protocol. There are no examples of success that people look for to prove our theories before believing something is possible.

I invite you to see yourself as a great scientist of our time. Imagine how little progress would have been made in the scientific field if all of them had doubted themselves and the theories that they conceptualized. Everything is harder to believe in, prior to physically seeing the evidence or proof of it; and it is part of our instinctual programming to always look for proof that something is true or "safe" prior to letting down our guard. This is why we hesitate to be the trailblazer and why so many watch to see what everyone else is doing so that we can then "follow the leader".

This is not behavior to be ashamed of or beat yourself up for succumbing to because it is inherent in how our subconscious works to protect us. When we recognize this behavior in ourselves however, we must choose a different action. Be aware that you will question yourself and any new, divinely inspired ideas that come to you. Be aware and have faith. Trust in your guidance.

You can choose to be the trailblazer that our world needs, voicing concern and working to change the norms when they are toxic and do not serve humanity.

Normalizing Trailblazing

Doing something new does not have to be hard, so I will share some tips to make this endeavor easier.

First, understand that it can be lonely. We are programmed to thrive in community, so as soon as possible you should explore recruiting at least one person to join you in your inspired idea vetting and plan creation.

Remember that not every inspired idea is meant to be created. Sometimes they are given to us to lead us somewhere new. Sometimes we are meant to expand on the concept or come across an entirely different idea as we are researching the first one. By recruiting at least one other person to brainstorm with you, you will be enlisting the power of a mastermind which will help you come up with new ideas or questions as part of the process. An additional benefit is the energy of coming together with another person for a common goal, which will help to fuel your passion and conviction for your path. It is also helpful to be part of a community of like-minded trailblazers. Even though your path is unique to you, it can be empowering to surround yourself with others who understand why you do what you do.

After you have a thinking partner, ensure that you stay open to any of their questions or suggestions. You do not have to adopt any of them but stay open to the possibilities. Quite often our guidance leads us to situations such as conversations, to help bring us to new understandings. Just stay open and continue to check-in with your inner wisdom on the way forward that is in your highest good. Note that your highest good may not be the quickest or simplest path; but it is the one you should be on, nonetheless.

The final step is to cultivate faith and trust in yourself and the plan you have put together. It could take time for you to see any results, so it is imperative that you believe in your inner wisdom and in yourself. And the way to instill hope in a positive outcome is to put that faith into action. That is all it takes.

Faith in action *creates hope* and more empowered actions.

When you share your hope and aligned, trailblazing action with others, you will inspire them to do something similar. Everyone looks for proof that something can be done, but they do not have to see a lot of people doing it. Your example could be all of the proof they need that it is possible. This will be especially true for those who know you best and can see the growth you have made. Those who see you in your new role as a trailblazer will know it is possible for them to change and blaze a trail as well.

Your action and the sharing of what you are doing, is how we will begin to normalize this behavior. You can be the proof that it is possible for others.

Domestic Struggles

At the time of this writing, there is a lot of chaos on political and economic fronts around the world. I am mentioning this because all of these areas intersect and impact how we treat our planet.

It is an instinctual response for people to focus on addressing an immediate fear or perceived threat before they can turn their attention to their ideals and create a better future. It is implicit in the state of our current reality, that you may struggle to turn your attention to the environment. The environment will continue to be our largest and most compelling threat; but because the repercussions seem like they are not as immediate, you will likely be called to focus your attention elsewhere.

If this scenario resonates, you should remember:

A. Do not feel guilty that you are distracted and focused on more domestic issues or crises.

B. Do not lose sight of what matters. Yes, you need to prioritize your immediate basic needs being met; but continuing to focus on day to day and not our future is what caused and continues to amplify the climate crisis.

C. Continue to give thought to this issue and do what you can, as soon as you can, no matter how small.

It will be an integral part of your leadership through these troubling times, to continue to acknowledge and stay aware of what both yourself and others may be going through. If they lose their job or are struggling to pay their bills, they will be deaf to other looming calamities and your efforts to incite action on climate change.

This particular deafness is not due to denial or a freeze response to the climate crisis, but is a survival instinct. We are programmed when in the midst of a perceived personal threat, for our brain to shut out distractions so that we can focus all of our attention on getting out of the current predicament.

This is another reason that the climate crisis continues to be ignored. Our world seems to be perpetually in crisis and you may feel like you have just put out one fire when another one springs forward and you must go into crisis management mode again.

My best advice here is to set your intention to manage your thoughts so that you are able to think clearly as you strategize and reassess your priorities. Remind your subconscious that you are not in physical danger, and practice a calming technique anytime you feel stress creeping in.

Review all of your concerns and reprioritize your action plan regularly. Reminding yourself that you are in fact taking action will create a feeling of more empowerment and lead to more inspiration for future actions.

I have used this technique successfully a few times in my life when the walls seemed to be closing in on me. Here are a few tips to keep you organized:

1. **Self-care** - This is over complicated and puts way too much burden on people who already have too much going on. If you do not have an hour or two to spend on yourself, do not try to find it. That just puts more stress on you. Practice focusing on your breath to calm your nerves and be proud of yourself for taking "a minute" to destress. It really is all you need.

2. **Brain dump** - There is something cathartic in taking all of that overwhelming list of items bashing around in your head, and getting it out of your head and onto paper. There are different parts of the brain involved when you put ideas in written form on paper, so that is what I recommend; but do not allow it to be a deal breaker if you prefer digital. You do not want to allow any resistance to stop you from conveying it all out of your head, so you can see it in one spot.

3. **Sit with it** - This does not have to be for long, although I recommend revisiting and updating your list often as new ideas and inspiration, or realizations come to you.

You may find that some of those items really are not that important, or some can be delegated which is a quick way to get them off your list for a "win". This is a working document so there should be no stress over any decisions made. You can always expand, delete or delegate more each time you circle back to it; you just want to feel organized and have a place to start.

4. **Prioritize** - You clearly only have so many hours in the day, so what needs to be done first? Making clear and reasonable decisions on the order and speed with which you can move through your list will take some of the pressure off of you. I also like to prioritize within the day, because I know there are certain times of day when my focus is better. I can tackle more complicated projects at those times and get more done.

5. **Revisit your priorities often** - Life happens and priorities must shift, but that does not mean that it has to completely derail you from your best laid plans.

One Step

The only way to approach substantive change is one step at a time. A big project can seem daunting and this is the only approach that works.

We must hold our vision of the outcomes desired and then back into the plans that we determine will get us there.

This translates into the first step being the creation of the vision of life in a new era of compassion. This requires an intricate analysis of all areas of life that must transform in order to support humanity in better ways, bringing our vision of a better world into fruition.

To reiterate the primary premise behind our prescribed actions, we are not being handed the prize of a golden era.

We must take action to create it.

We are entering the most exciting time in human history and we have the opportunity to craft our future into the most beautiful society and culture we can imagine.

It is truly a great gift and burdensome responsibility.

On one hand, we are creative beings and therefore fueled and fulfilled by the challenge of creating new things and circumstances.

And at the same time, we have a responsibility to craft a vision that will support our future generations and not just our immediate comfort and sensibilities. This is the rub of our current predicament.

Humans crave comfort which we find in consistency.

To ensure our survival and the betterment of humanity, however, it will require massive shifts in our behaviors and structures. These shifts, because they require change, will be highly uncomfortable for most people. Therefore these proposed changes will generate pervasive resistance throughout every level of society.

It's ironic. The first time the majority of earth's population may agree on something across all levels of its cultures, nations and socioeconomic groups, will be through their resistance to the actions necessary to save themselves.

Past efforts to transform humanity have included half hearted attempts at salvation, which imposed shifting into a celestial way of being rather than being human. It will not work like that.

We are here on earth to have a human experience. We have divinity within us but will always need to work in harmony with our humanness.

This is why most of the interpretations of a new earth or paradise on earth are inaccurate. We will experience this desired golden era while we are still living a human experience; and although the most transcendent emotions will be available to us, we will still need to live within the confines of the human body and who we are.

You have heard that we are made in God's image and similar to divinity in our desire to create and innovate. Now let us explore the beautiful attributes that make us uniquely human. These are some of the qualities that must be accounted for in the planning for an evolved existence and new era of raised consciousness.

We are a delightful, harmonious combination of both human and divine consciousness.

Our human aspect imbues us with a few charming characteristics that divinity does not hold. This is also why, even though we each have divinity within us, we are not deities ourselves.

1. This first one is the most obvious, but important to our planning. We are not eternal beings. We have a limited and relatively short time to enjoy our human experience. Lifespans will expand as we move into the next era, due in large part to reducing toxicity; but they will still be considered limited and our good health is to be cherished and nurtured while we are here.

2. We are emotional creatures. In the past this has worked against us, as we struggled to move past the more dense and unpleasant of human emotions. But as our frequencies ascend and we are better able to regulate those emotions, it opens the door to more of the transcendent emotions we want to experience such as love, joy and inner peace.

3. We are created to be tribal in our nature. Our ability to connect and bond with other humans is innate and part of our unique human experience. Being in community with others has the ability to lift our spirits, improve longevity and inspire us to be more fulfilled as we live in service to others.

4. Our nature is malleable, meaning that we are able to adapt and improve our identity and ways of being in the world. This ability to continuously grow and expand is mirrored from divinity, but applying this growth opportunity to our identity is uniquely human.

5. We are meant to be of service. We are each given an overriding purpose for our soul's journey, and it will always involve a way to be of service to others. We are

all meant to contribute to the greater good of humanity and…

When everyone responds to their calling, the world will be much richer both in circumstances and on an emotional plain of existence.

6. Turbulence and destruction serve no one and are outcomes of greed and a lack mentality. Humans are meant to experience abundance in all things and this is part of the joy that awaits us on the other side of our metamorphosis.

7. Humans have subconscious programs which are distinct to humanity AND we were given free choice which allows us the opportunity to learn how to override those programs that do not serve us. This is another growth opportunity that is inherently human.

It is an unfortunate myth that most of our societies have bought into, that our habitual behaviors and instincts can not be unlearned or reprogrammed. This process is part of the joy of being human and experiencing achievements. Most of the exciting goals we dream of accomplishing will require growth and new habits and it is distinctly rewarding to work through the obstacles necessary to create them.

A Great Vision, Broken Down

In order to create a better, evolved world with a healthy environment, it is a pivotal first step to cast a vision of this paradise. Once we can visualize it in intricate detail, it becomes easier to articulate and prioritize the steps and strategies that will be required to create this joyful realm of existence.

Let us start by outlining the categories that cannot be overlooked. The primary areas that must be nurtured for human happiness are:

Health and safety - Basic needs have to be met for every human around the globe. This includes universal healthcare, sanitation, nutrition, and shelter. And although violence will eventually be unheard of, there will be a transition period of several generations when security will also need to be provided.

Education - If we want to create a world of humanitarians and conscious stewards of the earth, changes have to start with how our youth are indoctrinated. Teaching them to embrace the joys of learning and growth rather than top grades and attempting perfection will be fundamental. In addition, skills such as creativity and exploration, dynamic systems analysis, emotional intelligence, collaboration and community building must be integrated into the fabric of education to guide who our future generations will become.

Earth Stewardship - This will not be a short term conversation. Responsible stewardship of the planet and all of God's creatures must be ongoing. As we continue to advance there will always be cross roads to navigate that impact and reverberate through other areas of our ecosystems. We can never again be insular in our approach to advancements. Progress will continue at an ever increasing rate and requires our diligence and wise stewardship.

Governmental Oversight - I believe I speak for the majority on the planet when I express a desire for less government regulation and oversight in our day to day lives. The complexities of living in harmony in our communities will involve some type of ongoing regulation and reward system, however. The inclusion of the global community in decision making will be necessary to ensure that we do not matriculate back into a culture of "have and have nots" depending on our geography.

Fiduciary Systems - At this point in our evolution, the world must continue to have a system of exchange for goods and services. In the future, these systems will need to develop into unilateral uniformity, to ensure a consistency in economy for all.

Articulating the vision in detail is beyond the scope of this book because it will involve the input and consensus of many, and the minutiae of a vision will vary by region.

The overriding value and vision required is that we experience and live in love for ourselves, humanity and all of the planet; and that we responsibly steward it and each other, as we enjoy our life experience.

That part is non-negotiable. The rest of the details will be up to us to create.

Faith In Action

It is true that there is not much with our current circumstances to inspire hope.

That is why it will serve you well to have faith.

The definition of hope is faith in action.

Faith can be defined as a belief in something that cannot be seen, and for the purpose of this narrative it includes having faith in the better world that we aspire to create.

Faith is holding the belief that a new era of raised consciousness, peace and love is possible and just waiting for us to co-create it.

And it may go without saying that the ultimate faith to help us through this period of chaos will be in Our Creator who, when we listen and allow it, is guiding us through these turbulent times.

When you develop a personal relationship with God, you will have a deep and reassuring knowing in your heart, as opposed to a cognitive understanding, that you are never alone; and you will be guided through life's tribulations.

A personal relationship and opportunity to guide us is all God wants of each of us.

All they want is a personal connection with you so that you can know their love at a deeper level, and benefit from their guidance that is always there for you.

As we have elaborated, some people refer to this connection or communication from God as their intuition or inner knowing. It is actually claircognizance and it is communication coming from your personal connection to Divinity. This is the part of you that is an extension from God and with you to love and guide you throughout your life. It is the part of you that hears your prayers. And it has been with you always, but most of us have been taught to doubt this inner wisdom or knowing as illogical; and so we ignore the guidance it shares with us.

When you are crystal clear that you are never alone and that God is with you, loving and guiding you always, there is no fear.

There is only faith in your direction and your yet unseen future.

You will have deep faith that you are taking the most aligned actions possible and that together as a global community we *will* be able to turn the tide.

We have talked a bit about your leadership and your ability to contribute to this peaceful revolution that the earth and humanity so desperately need; but you may recognize that there are many choices you will have to make moving forward.

At this juncture, it is helpful to recap the most pressing decisions you will need to make in determining your path forward. I hope you will take a few minutes to think about these prompts and document your answers, in order to create your next steps or an action plan.

1. Your first decision will be whether reading this narrative was to satiate a mild curiosity and you are ready to finish and walk away from its ideas OR

Are you ready to take a small next step to set a ripple in motion and help turn the tide?

Remember that the bigger your hesitation (which may be subconscious fear of stepping on toes or stirring conflict) the more important it will be to *start small right away.*

Don't wait for your thoughts to settle and your life to distract you from this important mission.

Our world needs you and your unique contributions to this cause. As you start taking very small actions, the subconscious resistance will begin to subside and it will become easier to take slightly bigger actions, and so on.

2.When can you allocate daily quiet time to tuning into your inner guidance and tapping into the deep well of wisdom that will lead you through this turbulent time? Remember that when you want to create a new habit, it is helpful to give yourself reminders and set aside time at the same time everyday so that it is easier to remember.

3. What type of additional information do you need in order to feel well informed and confident in sharing information?

I have included some vetted resources in the resource section. There are many other viable sources of information; but if internet searches are your best friend, please remember to vet your source of information. Most news sources are biased. As a place to start, look for scientific research or university studies.

4. Where is the low hanging fruit regarding your circle of influence? In other words, who will you be most comfortable conversing with about the changes needed to save our planet? Start with the easiest conversations first, in order to build your comfort level for broadening your scope.

5. Who would benefit from reading this book that you can share it with? Not everyone will be open to the spiritual concepts I have included. So although sharing a resource like this sounds like an easy step, it may not always be the most productive. If you have friends who are open minded, please share it so they can participate and lead in their own unique ways as well.

6.Who do you know that would never read this book but you could influence by having some non-threatening, information sharing conversations about climate change? No one has to have a close relationship with God to care about and be able to contribute to saving the planet.

Every person on this planet has skin in this game. If you know people who are not spiritual, you can still share the critical message about saving our environment.

BE FLEXIBLE in your approach and willing to listen to everyone's counter points if they have them. You could even share scientific articles to allow them to reach their own conclusions in their own time.

There is nothing to lose and everything to gain.

7. What timeframe will you give yourself to be accountable and start taking your first actions?

Who do you know that could be an accountability partner and join you in leading some aspect of this peaceful revolution in your community? Over 88% of the population does better with external accountability and/or a partner to help motivate them.

This earth stewardship role is probably a new identity for you and will create some resistance. Do not try to create a new habit or work through your fear or resistance alone. Take advantage of this instinctual desire for community and you will have more fun in the process, while you take inspired action with a friend.

8. Where is the least threatening point of entry for you? If you do not see yourself as the leader, can you see yourself as a friend with a mission to share and recruit others to? Or perhaps you are more of an organizer and boots on the ground advocate? Is there an aligned or accessible local organization that you can volunteer to help with, by donating your time in some manner?

9. What are your strongest skills to assist an environmental effort in some way? Or if you are run off your feet by life's responsibilities, who do you see in your daily routines that you can share information with; and how can you find some money on a regular basis to donate to an impactful environmental cause?

Your time on this planet is short, even without a climate

crisis that threatens to shorten it more. If you are still waffling on whether you should get involved in any way, ask yourself this question -

How will I feel about myself and my actions, when this crisis worsens and threatens our very existence; and I could have taken actions to help turn the tide but I did nothing?

The biggest disappointment of those reflecting on their lives just before leaving the planet, is regret for things not done. Regret that they did not do something more or behave in a different manner.

Do not let that be you.

The crescendo of the waves of destruction plummeting the planet with one disaster and crisis after another is deafening, but we are still at a tipping point where the tide can be turned. It is a bit like that saying about moving a mountain, however. One person alone cannot move that mountain.

But together, all of our small actions of resistance to the old toxic ways, combined with our new behaviors and advocacy for humanity and the planet, create a constantly growing ocean of ripples that has the power to turn the tide - or completely erode that mountain.

Together, our combined efforts have the power to save humanity from extinction…

**And escalate a rising tide of transformation
that will evolve into a new and**

Golden Era for humanity.

It all starts with you answering the call to help.

And with me.

And with our neighbors and community members.

Together, we can co-create a healthy,
vibrant planet full of love and community.

Endnotes

The following free additional resources have been made available to those interested in continuing their journey. This is our time to lead a peaceful revolution of love; and create a Golden Era for humanity.

Free Facebook Group** - Join the conversation, share resources and ideas for progress, ask questions or just be supportive of others. facebook.com/groups/leadershipnewera/

** As interest grows, we plan to orchestrate free accountability and mastermind groups to help everyone maintain their positive intentions and put them into action.

Related Trainings - Here you will find short trainings about developing your clair senses, measuring your frequency, improving your emotional intelligence, and the scale for levels of human consciousness. cynthiarivard.com/hope-free-resources

1 - I share some easy ways to get started developing your inner guidance on this book's resources web page: cynthiarivard.com/hope-free-resources

2 - "Deforestation and Climate Change," Climate Council, December 10, 2024,   climatecouncil.org.au/deforestation

3 - Emily Cassidy, "Emissions from Fossil Fuels Continue to Rise," NASA Earth Observatory, re: 2023 data. earthobservatory.nasa.gov/images/152519/emissions-from-fossil-fuels-continue-to-risebook

4 - I mention the benefit of developing your inner knowing in numerous contexts throughout the book. You can access a free, short video training about this concept here: cynthiarivard.com/hope-free-resources

5 - I have included an abbreviated version of the scale of consciousness here. You will notice that the most unpleasant emotions resonate at the lower end of this frequency scale. They are heavier, denser emotions and when we feel them strongly or for an extended period the energy of that emotion can become trapped in our body or auric field.

Scale of Consciousness

Bio-energy units	Consciousness level
500 million	Joyful
400 million	Unconditionally loving
25 million	Abundant
250,000	Creative
100,000	Purposeful
25,000	Altruistic
8000	Courageous
1200	Content
800	Lazy
500	Disillusioned
250	Grieving, Arrogant
200	Angry, Hateful
150	Apathetic, Fearful
100	Guilty, Hopeless
20	Shameful

Remember that everything is energy and energy is supposed to flow. Typically, the energy of the emotions we feel will dissipate quickly. When they become trapped they can cause both physical or mental disease. Or you may just feel heavier with that particular energy hanging with you after your thoughts have moved on and you are no longer conscious of feeling it.

And these trapped emotions will keep your frequency from rising. In most instances, an energy master can quickly dissipate these trapped emotions. We do this online in group settings every month in the Rising Tide Donor Community.

Because humans are emotional creatures, having emotions become trapped is normal, so I recommend that you check on this regularly to keep energy flowing as it is meant to.

6 - You can also access a free short training on how to measure your frequency and receive a copy of the scale of human consciousness at the book resource web page.

7 - See endnote 4 for the abbreviated scale of consciousness.

8 - See endnote 4 above.

9 - Emotional intelligence - increasing your emotional intelligence is an ongoing practice and skill set that can always be honed. Learning to regulate your emotions will contribute to the speed with which you are able to raise your consciousness.

The two are very similar, however you can raise your EQ without raising your consciousness, A raised consciousness requires that your vibration be raised first.

As your frequency and consciousness rises, it becomes easier to regulate your emotions, but this is still a skill that requires awareness and intentionality.

 Let us assume that she has a horrible habit of talking over you and trying to tell you what to do. Your feelings or reaction to this has nothing to do with her. It is the interpretation that you are putting on her behavior.

Tips for emotional regulation:

- Start by increasing your awareness. Make a point of checking in with yourself multiple times throughout the day to determine what emotion you're feeling. If you notice an unpleasant emotion, try to determine what your thoughts were that preceded that emotion.> Your thoughts create your emotions.

- Think about when you notice an unpleasant emotion. Are there patterns or similarities in your thoughts that created them? Are there common types of triggers? An example of this might be a desire to control people or outcomes, or a need to be right.

- Look for patterns and then think of ways that you can reframe these thoughts. The important concept to recognize in order for this to work is that if you do not like a particular emotion that you are feeling, you must change your thought.

- Then practice changing your thought patterns, especially around any specific triggers that you have been able to identify. As an example, if you notice a growing angst when you are about to visit your mother in law, identify the point of stress. Let us assume that she has a horrible habit of talking over you and trying to tell you what to do. Your feelings or reaction to this

- has nothing to do with her. It is the interpretation that you are putting on her behavior.

  You may be thinking that she does not trust you, value what you have to say or believe you are able to get things done without her direction. A reframe of these thoughts could be that she has low self-esteem and developed this behavior to convince herself that she has value to offer.

  Do you see the difference in those two perceptions? One leads to aggravation and the other to compassion. Always adopt the viewpoint that leads to the most compassion.

  Finally, praise yourself for your efforts and continually look for new areas where you can uplevel this skill. It requires practice and diligence.

10 - John Bateman, "2024 Was the World's Warmest Year on Record," National Oceanic and Atmospheric Administration, US Dept. of Commerce, Jan. 10, 2025

11 - "How Climate Change Impacts Marine Life," European Environment Agency, Nov. 30, 2023

12) This is channeled information the author received and cannot currently be validated by scientific research. Current scientific projections have not yet taken into account the accelerating trajectory we are now seeing.

13) John Bateman, "2024 Was the World's Warmest Year on Record," NOAA, US Dept. of Commerce, Jan. 10, 2025

14) "Global Climate Highlights 2024," Copernicus, Jan. 10, 2025

15) "Rising Ocean Temperatures are Leading to Historic Coral Bleaching," Environment America, April 15, 2024

16) "The Effects of Deforestation," Climate Impact Partners, Nov. 28, 2024,

17) See endnote 9.

Resources

Articles

To begin, the United Nations offers a plethora of unbiased educational resources on their website. un.org/en/climatechange

The European Environment Agency also offers an abundance of information and data as well as links to additional articles and publications: eea.europa.eu/en

NASA also offers quite a bit of information on different aspects of climate change along with facts and statistics on their website: science.nasa.gov/climate-change

Vetted Charities & Environmental Groups

These charitable organizations are either volunteer run, or transparent in how their donations are allocated. Their use of funds are streamlined and effective in creating the impact that is intended.

Stewarding into the New Era will require each of us to

donate our time, talent and treasures in new and more significant ways. This is not an exhaustive list, and everyone is encouraged to do their own research and give generously in the ways and areas to which you are guided to contribute. I will host an updated list on my website, adding additional worthwhile organizations as they come to my attention.

Charity Water - Works to end the global clean water crisis. charitywater.org

Doctors Without Borders - Provides medical humanitarian assistance to people who need it most. doctorswithoutborders.org

Earth Justice - The premiere nonprofit public interest environmental law organization, here because the earth needs a good lawyer. earthjustice.org

Eden Projects - Partners with communities to restore degraded landscapes, creating sustainable ecosystems that benefit both people and the environment. eden-plus.org

The Greener Earth Project - They are planting trees to support the offset of carbon on climate change. thegreenerearthproject.org

The Institute of Global Homelessness - Is driving a global movement to end street homelessness. ighomelessness.org

MedShare International - A U.S. based organization that recovers unused medical resources to redistribute to underserved global communities. medshare.org

Oceana - is the largest international advocacy organization focused on ocean conservation. oceana.org

Pachamama Alliance - A global community that offers training and connection focused on climate activism and creating a sustainable future. pachamama.org

Purpose on the Planet Foundation - This organization is making a difference by planting mangrove trees to reduce poverty and offset carbon emissions. purposeontheplanet.org

Shelter Box - Their mission is to build awareness of global displacement and to facilitate providing families with life-saving shelter and essential tools and supplies. shelterboxusa.org

Sierra Club - U.S. based environmental group dedicated to enjoying, exploring and protecting the wild places of the earth. sierraclub.org

The Water Project - Provides access to clean, safe and reliable water across sub-Saharan Africa. thewaterproject.org

Woods Hole Oceanographic Institute - Is the world's leading, independent non-profit organization dedicated to ocean research, exploration, and education. whoi.edu

World Animal Protection - A global organization with a mission to end animal cruelty and suffering. worldanimalprotection.org

World Housing Organization - Working toward a vision of providing housing for all. worldhousing.org

Author Bio

Cynthia Rivard is a spiritual teacher, business advisor and environmental advocate. Through a meteoric upleveling of channeling skills, she has become a crystal clear seer for awakening humanity to the next chapter of its evolution. Raising consciousness and saving humanity from extinction due to the effects of climate change are the first priority.

After a long career in executive leadership, Cynthia believes in the power of heart centered communication and egoless leadership to drive improvements in society. When the world is governed by individuals who focus on the good of all, the earth will come to know peace, prosperity and a healthy environment.

Cynthia has established a web page with resources for building your conscious leadership and skills to be the change you care about at: cynthiarivard.com/hope-free-resources/

She is the founder of the Global Rising Tide Foundation, which is a movement of individuals and responsible corporate partners who are committed to stewarding the earth, raising consciousness, and creating innovative solutions to support humanity into its next era.

Additional Books by Cynthia Rivard

The Golden Era Creation Series encapsulates a message of hope, love and transformation as well as guidance for the inspired action necessary to ensure humanity's survival and ultimate transition into our promised next chapter of evolution – The Golden Era.

Book One - *"Hope For A New Era"*

More to come in the ***Golden Era Creation Series:***

Book Two (release Nov. 2025) - *"Golden Era Rising: A Guide for Personal and Global Upleveling"* – In book two, the overwhelming task of creating the new era is broken down into manageable actions, tips and strategies that can embolden you to get started now. You will learn how to manifest your own transcendent joy and assist in the co-creation of a golden future for the planet and our species.

Book Three - *"A Divine Beginning, God's Promise for Humanity's Golden Era"* – In book three, the author channels a clear message of hope and inspiration from Divinity. It illuminates our evolutionary history, lessons that can be learned and a reminder of our Great Creator's love and desire for our happiness. God/Allah/ Spirit is with us always and guiding us to co-create the bright next phase of our evolutionary journey – our Golden Era.

The Revolution Series

A revolution is a movement to create momentous change for the better. In this series the author enumerates the key areas for healing humanity. We are in uncertain and unprecedented times that call for new ways of being and operating.

Book One(release Sept. 2025) - "A New Breed of Leader" is a guide for healing the rift and leading peaceful revolution. Calming the chaos requires each of us to join the conversation and take action to propel the creation of peace and prosperity. You will learn how to navigate contentious topics, build consensus to create progress and nurture communities where everyone can flourish. These skills will carry over to everywhere in life. Now more than ever, we must build bridges instead of walls.

More to come in The Revolution Series

Book Two - *"A New Breed of Business" continues the leadership conversation in a narrative that inspires better business. This hands on manual for the necessary transitions will guide business owners and leaders step by step through their metamorphosis for serving humanity in more expansive ways.*

Book Three - "A New Breed of Governance" is a realistic review of the metamorphosis our global societies must make if we are to live in harmony. Starting with the micro level of community leadership, this go-to-guide outlines goals and strategies for an equitable transition to "humanity first" governance.

www.ingramcontent.com/pod-product-compliance
Lightning Source LLC
LaVergne TN
LVHW052023080426
835513LV00018B/2135